ENJOYING

TEQUILA

Brimming with creative inspiration, how-to projects, and useful information to enrich your everyday life, Quarto Knows is a favorite destination for those pursuing their interests and passions. Visit our site and dig deeper with our books into your area of interest: Quarto Creates, Quarto Cooks, Quarto Homes, Quarto Lives, Quarto Drives, Quarto Explores, Quarto Gifts, or Quarto Kids.

© 2021 Quarto Publishing Group USA Inc.

First Published in 2021 by Voyageur Press, an imprint of The Quarto Group, 100 Cummings Center, Suite 265-D, Beverly, MA 01915, USA. T (978) 282-9590 F (978) 283-2742 QuartoKnows.com

Voyageur Press titles are also available at discount for retail, wholesale, promotional, and bulk purchase. For details, contact the Special Sales Manager by email at specialsales@quarto.com or by mail at The Quarto Group, Attn: Special Sales Manager, 100 Cummings Center, Suite 265-D, Beverly, MA 01915, USA.

25 24 23 22 21   1 2 3 4 5

ISBN: 978-0-7603-7507-5

Digital edition published in 2021
eISBN: 978-0-7603-7508-2

Library of Congress Cataloging-in-Publication Data is available

Design and Page Layout: Ashley Prine, Tandem Books
Cover Frame: Vasya Kobelev/Shutterstock
Cover Illustration: MoreVector/Shutterstock
Interior Illustrations and Photography: See page 176

Printed in China

ENJOYING TEQUILA

A TASTING GUIDE AND JOURNAL

PAUL KAHAN

CONTENTS

TASTING NOTES

INTRODUCTION

Welcome to *Enjoying Tequila: A Tasting Guide and Journal*. In the following pages you will discover the secrets to fully appreciating Mexico's complex and enigmatic national drink. Born from the collision of ancient Aztec religious practice and European distillation technology, tequila has been embraced, but often misunderstood, by the rest of the world. In the centuries since Spanish settlers established Mexico's first distilleries, traditional methods of growing, harvesting, and processing the blue agave plant have merged with cutting-edge technology to supply a growing thirst for tequila. This book chronicles tequila's history, breaking down myths and demonstrating the truth is sometimes stranger than fiction. Find out how blue agaves are transformed into tequila and get answers to questions like, "What's the deal with worms in tequila bottles?" and "Is it true that tequila can be turned into diamonds?"

By reading this book, you will also learn how to interpret a tequila bottle's label like a pro, so you can properly identify brands and styles. More importantly, you will come to appreciate the myriad of flavors and aromas that tequila has to offer; you'll discover what to focus on when sipping tequila so you enjoy it like a connoisseur. Finally, you will visit some of Mexico's oldest and best-known tequila distilleries and producers to grasp what makes them so popular and respected. If you sip as you read this book, you'll really get a baseline for appreciating tequila that will help you develop your own taste for this unique liquor. I hope you enjoy your journey into the world of Mexico's national spirit!

A BRIEF
HISTORY

A DRINK FOR THE GODS

Tequila's origins stretch back more than three millennia. Around 1000 BCE, more than two centuries before the founding of Rome, Aztecs living in what is today southern Mexico began fermenting sap from maguey (a grass-like flowering plant that generally grows in high-altitude regions that are hot and arid, such as Mexico and the southwestern United States) to create a drink called *pulque*, a milky white drink with a sour taste. Pulque was initially closely associated with the Aztec goddess Mayahuel, whose name is reminiscent of maguey. According to Aztec tradition, Mayahuel was the goddess of fertility and had four hundred breasts to feed each of her four hundred children. This was far from the Aztecs'

only use for maguey; they also used the plant for food, clothing, and musical instruments.

Though initially considered to be a sacred drink, by the time the Spanish arrived in Mexico in the sixteenth century, consumption of pulque was widespread among all classes of Aztecs. The Spanish conquistadors did not like pulque and, when they ran out of their stores of brandy, set about experimenting with alternatives. Using their copper stills, the Spanish began distilling maguey. They called the result *vino de mezcal* ("oven-cooked agave"). These distillation operations were often quite primitive. For instance, Tecuane Canyon, which is about three miles outside Amatitán, is home to the ruins of an old taberna, or shop, where tequila was distilled on-site. Built sometime during the 1600s, the site has a large round pit in which the agave hearts were cooked on the embers of a wood fire. Later in the process, the mezcal was fermented in pits carved into the tepetate rock large enough for a person to climb into! According to American ethnographer Edward S. Curtis, who observed Mescalero Apache Indians distilling mezcal in the early twentieth century, "The Indians say its taste is sharp, like whiskey. A small quantity readily produces intoxication." Initially, mezcal production was a small-scale, local affair, with the agave's piñas (the heart of the plants) being fermented in simple clay pots.

VINO MEZCAL DE TEQUILA

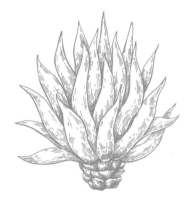

One variety of mezcal, made from the blue maguey plant, came to be called *tequila* after the town in which it was produced. Tequila, in the present-day Mexican state of Jalisco, means "volcanic rock" or "rock that cuts" in an Aztec dialect known as Nahuatl. The region's volcanic soil was silicate rich, which helped blue maguey thrive while the vino de mezcal produced there soon earned a reputation for being especially high quality. The first mention of vino de mezcal production in Tequila dates to 1608. Not surprisingly, Tequila became the sight of the first large-scale distillery in Mexico. In the 1600s, Mexican aristocrat Pedro Sánchez de Tagle, 2nd Marquis of Altamira, built a distillery at his Hacienda Cuisillos to create vino de mezcal. Don Pedro was born in Spain in 1661 and migrated to Mexico, where he created vino de mezcal from the locally abundant blue maguey. The size of Don Pedro's distillery made tequila ubiquitous in Mexico and earned for him the title "father of tequila."

However, success attracts imitators, and by the eighteenth century, several families had entered the vino de mezcal de tequila business. The most prominent of these was Don José Antonio de Cuervo, of whom little is known. Apparently, he operated a

A PLANT FOR ALL SEASONS

The agave is a remarkably resilient plant, capable of surviving temperatures as low as 15 degrees Fahrenheit and as high as 105! Though native to a relatively small portion of the planet, they grow in a variety of terrains, including plains, deserts, and forests. As far back as 7000 BCE, the Aztecs used the agave plant for food, medicine, drink, and clothing, leading the Spanish to dub it "El Árbol de las Maravillas," or "the tree of wonders."

tavern called La Chorrera (a term that means "stream" and may have denoted "waterfall") around 1740 that produced mezcal and sold it to travelers and the locals. In 1758, Don José received a grant of land near Tequila from Spain's King Ferdinand VI (1713–1759) to grow blue maguey (by now called agave, based on the Greek word *agauē*, which means "illustrious" or "brilliant"). Don José purchased the property from Vicente de Saldivar, who had already constructed a tequila distillery on the site. Unfortunately for the Cuervo family, the following year King Ferdinand VI died and his successor, King Carlos III (1759–1788), issued a ban in 1788 on the production of several dozen alcoholic beverages, including mezcal. This curtailed, but did not exactly end, the Cuervo family's mezcal production for a decade (they simply moved production underground). In 1795, Carlos III's successor, King Carlos IV, issued to Don José's son, José María Guadalupe de Cuervo, a permit to manufacture vino de mezcal de tequila, and production soared.

When José Guadalupe died in 1812, the distillery became part of the dowry his daughter, María Magdalena Ignacia de Cuervo, brought into her marriage to Vicente Albino Rojas. It was Rojas who turned the distillery into an empire, cultivating approximately three million agave plants at the time of his death and exporting the family's tequila across Mexico. In fact, Fábrica La Rojeña (Rojas renamed the distillery

after marrying María Magdalena) is Latin America's oldest distillery and one of the continent's most successful. In 1889, Mexico's president, Porfirio Díaz, awarded the distillery a gold medal, which it celebrates to this day. Ironically, during the Mexican Revolution (a fight against President Díaz's unpopular regime that began in 1910 and continued for a decade), nationalists embraced tequila as an authentically Mexican drink, leading to a spike in its popularity. Today, a bottle of tequila is a traditional gift for departed ancestors during Mexico's national Day of the Dead celebration.

CROSSING THE BORDER

Interestingly, a former Cuervo employee would become one of that company's biggest and most important competitors. Born in 1842 in Jalisco, Don Cenobio Sauza settled in Tequila as a teenager and began working at Cuervo's distillery, where he learned how to cultivate blue agave and distill it into vino de mezcal de tequila. Seeing the profit to be made from the product, Sauza began exporting various distilleries' tequila, but in 1870 he leased his own facility, La Gallardeña, which proved enormously successful. In 1873, Sauza purchased a distillery

TEQUILA, A WORLD HERITAGE SITE

In 2006, the United Nations declared more than eighty-six thousand acres of land near Tequila, known as "the Agave Landscape and the Ancient Industrial Facilities of Tequila," a World Heritage Site. According to the United Nations, "Between the foothills of the Tequila Volcano and the deep valley of the Rio Grande River, is part of an expansive landscape of blue agave, shaped by the culture of the plant used since the 16th century to produce tequila spirit and for at least 2,000 years to make fermented drinks and cloth."

called La Antigua Cruz ("The Old Cross") and renamed it La Perseverancia ("Perseverance"), which is generally considered the founding of Sauza Tequila. The company grew quickly, in no small part due to being the first tequila producer to export to the United States. In fact, Americans' awareness of tequila got a further boost in 1893 when the agave plant was featured at the World's Columbian Exposition in Chicago, which attracted approximately twenty-seven million visitors. Those visitors who saw the plant read about its various products, including pulque and mezcal (which the *New York World* described as "an intoxicant more fiery than Jersey lightning," which was a popular hard cider). By about this time, most consumers referred to it as "tequila," rather than "mezcal de tequila."

Interestingly, during the (inaccurately named) Spanish flu pandemic of 1918, doctors actually prescribed tequila mixed

TEQUILA: A GIRL'S BEST FRIEND?

In November 2008, physicists working at the National Autonomous University of Mexico announced a discovery that sounded like it had been ripped from the pages of a bad science-fiction novel: They had turned tequila into diamonds! The team of scientists had been working to create inexpensive diamonds for industrial use (such as electrical insulators). During the course of their experiments, they placed a solution of 60 percent water and 40 percent ethanol on stainless steel trays, superheated the mixture, and observed the formation of diamond films. One of the scientists remarked that the solution's ratio of water and alcohol was the same as tequila's. According to Luis Miguel Apátiga, "To dissipate any doubts, one morning on the way to the lab I bought a pocket-size bottle of cheap white tequila and we did some tests. We were in doubt over whether the great amount of chemicals present in tequila, other than water and ethanol, would contaminate or obstruct the process, but it turned out to be not so. The results were amazing, same as with the ethanol and water compound, we obtained almost spherical shaped diamonds of nanometric size. There is no doubt; tequila has the exact proportion of carbon, hydrogen and oxygen atoms necessary to form diamonds." However, before you set fire to your tequila, remember that the diamonds that the physicists were able to create were tiny—they can only be seen with an electron microscope! In other words, you're still on the hook for two months' salary!

with lemon and salt as a cure for the illness's symptoms, which increased the drink's popularity. (Today, Mexicans often mix tequila in hot tea with lemon as a remedy for sore throats.) Ironically, Prohibition—the period during which the sale, manufacture, and distribution of alcohol was illegal in the United States (1920–1933)—was a boon to the tequila industry. Because American distillers were unable (in theory, at least) to produce liquor, consumers in the United States started importing spirits manufactured abroad. Mexico, sharing a nearly two-thousand-mile border with the United States, was ideally placed to smuggle alcohol into its northern neighbor. Americans flocked across the border, where they could drink legally, and many developed a taste for tequila. Of course, tequila also found its way into the southeastern United States and beyond.

The repeal of Prohibition did little to diminish Americans' taste for tequila, due in no small part to the popularity of a new drink: the margarita. Similar to a drink known as the daisy, the margarita (which is Spanish for "daisy") substituted tequila for brandy. The margarita's exact origins are obscure, but it was certainly established in the United States by the late 1930s, appearing in places such as California and Texas. At about this same time, Jose Cuervo became a leading brand in the United States when it was purchased by Heublein Spirits, an American liquor company that owned Smirnoff Vodka, Bass Ale, Bell's Whisky, and A.1. Steak Sauce. Cuervo's growing popularity

helped spur Americans' appetites for margaritas; in 1945, the company even ran advertisements with the slogan, "Margarita: It's More Than a Girl's Name." In December 1953, *Esquire* magazine published what is generally considered the first known recipe for a margarita, telling readers, "She's from Mexico, Senores, and her name is the Margarita Cocktail—and she is lovely to look at, exciting and provocative." In 2012, Nick Nicora of Ovations Food Services and Ricardo Hussong of Hussong's Cantina created the world's largest margarita at that year's California State Fair in Sacramento, California. Clocking in at 10,500 gallons, it contained 2,100 gallons of Jose Cuervo Especial Gold tequila (nearly 5,000 bottles) and was blended in a custom-made twenty-five-foot blender.

Needless to say, the fact that the United States was home to the world's largest margarita is proof that Americans love their tequila. Today, the United States is the number one market for tequila, consuming approximately 46 percent of the total amount

"WAITER, THERE'S A WORM IN MY TEQUILA!"

Actually, no there's not. The worms are called "maguey worms," but they are not actually worms at all: They are edible caterpillars that live on the agave plant. These larvae consume the agave plants and then become butterflies known as *Agave hesperiaris*, or the tequila giant skipper. There are two varieties of maguey worms bottled with mezcal, distinguished by color: the red (which lives in the agave's root piña) and the whitish gold (which lives on the agave's leaves). The former turns pale in the mezcal while the latter becomes gray. Bottles containing the worm are called "con gusano," and the ones bottled in mezcal are often cultivated specifically for this purpose. The exact origin of placing the maguey worms in bottles of mezcal is unclear, with some suggesting that distillers believe that it improved the mezcal's flavor while others claim that it testified to the high alcohol content (demonstrated by the liquid's ability to pickle the worm). During the 1940s, there was even a rumor that the maguey worms were an aphrodisiac or had magical properties. Maguey worms are never put into tequila (Mexican law prohibits it), only with other forms of mezcal, so if you find a maguey worm in your shot glass, you can be sure you are not actually drinking tequila.

distilled each year (in 2001, the Consejo Regulador del Tequila [CRT] even opened an office in Washington, DC, a mark of the significance of the US market for tequila). Moreover, the market has grown by an average of more than 6 percent each year for the last twenty years. Mexico is the number two market, accounting for about 40 percent of tequila consumption, with the rest of the world accounting for the balance.

PROTECTING THE BRAND

In late 1974, Mexico's Secretary of Industry and Commerce declared that the term *tequila* "shall be applied only to the alcoholic beverage known with the same name as referred to in the 'Quality Official Standard for Tequila,' as established by the General Direction for Standards of the Secretary of Heritage and Industrial Development." This declaration spelled out what raw materials could be used in making tequila and limited production to certain municipalities within the state of Jalisco. In particular, only distillations of a single variety of agave—*Agave tequilana* 'Weber Azul'—can claim to be tequila. Mexico registered tequila with the World Industrial Property Organization, a specialized agency of the United Nations tasked with promoting worldwide recognition and protection of copyrights and trademarks. This move essentially made tequila the intellectual property of Mexico and thereby prevented mezcals produced in other places from describing themselves as such.

During the 1990s, the Norma Oficial Mexicana (NOM) issued guidelines for production and labeling of tequila. Mexico's government then granted to the CRT the authority to enforce these regulations and standards and to combat corruption and forgery. (Founded in 1994 by the Chamber of Tequila Makers, the CRT is a private, nonprofit

WHAT'S IN A NAME?

Mexican regulations specify that tequila must be distilled from a single variety of agave: Weber Azul, or *Agave tequilana*. Most of that name is pretty straightforward: Agave is the plant's name, Tequilana is the region where it's found, and azul is the Spanish word for "blue." But who or what is Weber? The answer is Frédéric Albert Constantin Weber, a nineteenth-century French botanist. Weber served as a French military physician in Mexico between 1864 and 1867 (the French had installed Austrian Archduke Ferdinand Maximilian on the Mexican throne and the French military was there to support the would-be emperor). Though primarily a specialist in cacti (an entire genus of cacti, the *Weberocereus*, is named after him), Weber also identified several species of agave, including tequila's blue agave.

organization.) Meanwhile, in 1995, the Mexican government granted a Denominación de Origen to Oaxaca (in southern Mexico) for mezcal, which today accounts for 70 percent of the world's production, with most (approximately three quarters) being distilled from *Agave angustifolia* 'Espadín,' which has a comparatively high natural sugar content and reaches maturity relatively quickly.

MAKING
TEQUILA

Jose Cuervo

ALAMBIQUE
N°2
AP. 10,000 LTS.

LONG LIVE AGAVE

Tequila starts with the blue agave, one of more than 150 individual varieties of agave in Mexico. Though it resembles a cactus, the agave plant is in fact a succulent (it is similar to the lily), and the blue agave grows to between four and six feet tall with leaves that extend more than three feet from the plant's stem, or "heart" (most farmers cut the plant's leaves with a machete to protect it from insect infestation and to allow separate plants to grow closer together). Agave plants are asexual and are chiropterophilous, which is a fancy way of saying they reproduce by bats. The agave plants flower at night and give off a strong odor akin to rotting fruit. The musky smell attracts bats, which drink the agave plant's nectar and become covered in the plant's pollen and offshoots, carrying them to new locations. Cultivators plant agave offshoots in Mexico's rainy season (June through September) to allow the plants to absorb as much water as possible to sustain them during the long dry season. It takes approximately five to eight years for cultivated

agave plants to mature (and more than a decade for wild plants), and mature plants are harvested between January and May. There are currently more than twenty thousand cultivators tending more than four hundred million agave plants in and around Jalisco.

The Heart of the Matter

Instead of scraping out the agave's sap, as the Aztecs did, the Spanish extracted the piña (the plant's heart); today, this is done by farmers called *jimadors* using long-handled knives similar to machetes called *coa de jimas* (usually referred to simply as a "coa"). The piña, which vaguely resembles a pineapple, accounts for about one-half the agave plant's mass and weighs anywhere between 80 and 200 pounds. A typical jimador's day involves four to six hours harvesting one hundred piñas, which not only is backbreaking labor but also can be extremely hazardous: Snakes and tarantulas often settle under the agave plant's leaves and are none too happy to be disturbed by the jimador's coa!

The jimadors then halve or quarter the piñas to ensure consistent cooking in the steam-heated masonry ovens, known

NEVER TOUCH ANOTHER MAN'S COA

A jimador's coa de jima is not simply another tool; it is key to the jimador's livelihood, offers protection against animal attack, and is often used for several years. One expert has called a jimador's coa "a very personal item."

as *hornos*, that convert the sap into fermentable sugar. The jimadors bake the piñas for a day or two and then let them cool for anywhere between sixteen and forty-eight hours. The cooking process breaks down the piñas' inulin into fructose, or fruit sugar, which can be fermented into alcohol. Uncooked, the piña tastes something like a raw potato. In recent decades, some distilleries have turned to autoclaves, which use pressurized steam to cook the piñas more quickly than does an horno. The problem is that fast cooking increases the chances of burning the piñas' sugars, leaving the tequila with a caramel taste. Moreover, some tasters claim that, even when done properly, steam-oven-cooked agaves produce tequila with notes of leather, which is hardly something appealing to most drinkers.

After the piñas are cooled, the distilleries crush them to release the liquid sugar, called *aguamiel*. In the early days of distillation, distillers used a mill called a *tahona* to crush the piñas. A tahona is

OLD-SCHOOL TRENDSETTER?

Though Sauza Tequila is one of Mexico's oldest large-scale tequila distilleries, it has embraced a new method of processing agave. Instead of cooking the agave in hornos or autoclaves, a time-consuming process, Sauza Tequila crushes raw piñas and then dumps them into what is called a *bagasse bed*. The distillery then dumps water onto the crushed piñas, which absorbs the agave's inulin. The sugar-saturated water is drained off from the bagasse bed, combined with sulfuric acid to lower its pH, and then heated to convert the inulin to fermentable sugar. This process requires fewer employee-hours to produce a bottle of tequila, but is extremely controversial, with some tequila enthusiasts claiming it strips the final product of the complex flavors found in other brands. A slowly fermented tequila will usually take on notes of butter or dill, but shortcuts can leave the tequila with a raw agave taste that some people find off-putting.

a circular pit with a post in the center around which a giant stone wheel revolves. Prior to the twentieth century, mules or oxen were used to power the wheel, though most distilleries have abandoned the tahona in favor of conveyor belt–fed steam rollers powered by electricity (Patrón, which continues to use a tahona, is a notable exception). Distillers filter the resulting juice through a *pachaquil*, which strains out solid pieces of the piña and other debris. Today, three hundred million blue agave plants are harvested annually to satisfy Mexico and the United States' thirst for tequila.

Fermentation

The next step in the process is fermentation, or the use of microorganisms like yeast or bacteria to convert aguamiel's sugar into alcohol. Typically, distillers use yeast to ferment their aguamiel, breaking it down into carbon dioxide and ethyl alcohol, which is the active ingredient in alcoholic beverages. It is at this point in the process that cane or corn sugars will be added to create "mixto tequila," or those that are less than 100 percent blue agave. To legally be termed tequila, at least 51 percent of the fermentable sugar must be derived from agave. Some distillers produce 100 percent agave tequila (which is usually more expensive than mixto), while requiring that only agave sugars be fermented. Even at this late stage, there are many important decisions to be made that will affect the final

product's taste, color, and feel. For instance, distilleries use different forms of yeast to achieve the specific tastes and colors that distinguish their brands, and ferment the aguamiel in open or close vats made of wood or stainless steel. The fermentation process typically spans one to four days and produces a liquid, called "mosto," of between 7 and 12 proof.

Distilling, Aging, and Type

After fermentation, the mosto needs to be distilled at least twice. Distillation is a process that alternates boiling and condensation in copper or stainless steel stills, which concentrates the mosto, thereby increasing its alcohol by volume (ABV). The first distillation creates *ordinario*, which is approximately 50 proof, while the second creates tequila, which clocks in around 80 proof. (In Mexico, tequila for domestic consumption can be made as low as 38 proof, though US law requires any tequila sold in the United States to be at least 40 proof.) This tequila is clear and can be sold as *blanco* or *silver*. However, distillers also age their tequilas in oak or white oak barrels. The tannins in the oak change the

DOES IT COME BY THE SHOT?

In 2010, distillery Hacienda La Capilla released a 1.3-liter bottle of seven-year-old, 100 percent blue agave tequila. The price tag? A whopping $3.5 million, largely due to the 4,000 diamonds encrusting the five-pound platinum bottle designed by Mexican artist Fernando Altamirano. It was exhibited around the world and trumpeted as "a jewel enveloping another jewel." Dubbed the "Diamond Sterling," it replaced the earlier winner of the coveted title "World's Most Expensive Bottle of Tequila." According to the Guinness World Records, in 2006, a platinum-and-white-gold bottle of six-year-old, 100 percent blue agave tequila was auctioned for $225,000.

TO YOUR HEALTH!

A medical study released in 2014 had tequila enthusiasts cheering: Agave could help you lose weight! With all things, though, the devil is in the details: In a laboratory study with rats, a sweetener created from agave's inulin did not increase blood glucose levels in the way that other forms of sugar do. However, the rats did not sip tequila; instead, the scientists administered water infused with agave sugar (known as "agavins"). Due to the distillation process, tequila does not have any agavins and drinking it is not recommended as a weight loss strategy. Nevertheless, inulin has been used to sweeten candy, yogurt, ice creams, and sauces, mostly in Europe and Japan. That's not all! A 2010 report from the American Chemical Society suggested that the blue agave's *fructans* (a chain of fructose molecules) might help prevent osteoporosis, and other studies have shown that tequila itself (rather than the blue agave) might help lower cholesterol and that the drink acts as an aperitif, stimulating digestion and the metabolism. There's even some anecdotal evidence that a shot of tequila might help alleviate migraines.

tequila's flavor, mellowing it. Tequila aged for up to a year in an oak barrel is called *reposado* (Spanish for "rested"), while tequila aged for between one and three years is called *añejo* ("vintage"). The longer a tequila is aged, the more of the barrel's color it absorbs, becoming darker yellow. Some distillers mix blanco with either aged tequilas or colorants and sweeteners designed to soften the alcohol's taste; these are called "joven" or "gold" tequilas. Since 2005, distilleries have offered *extra añejo*, defined as tequila that has aged for more than three years. For both reposado and añejo tequilas, the CRT vigorously monitors distilleries' aging protocols by sealing the barrels.

* * *

READING
A LABEL

DEFINING TEQUILA

Mexico's Consejo Regulador del Tequila (CRT) defines tequila as a fermented drink composed of at least 51 percent of "total reducer sugars . . . extracted from the Agave *tequilana Weber variedad azul* grown within the territory defined in the Declaration." Furthermore, to legally be defined as tequila, it must "be bottled in packing facilities located within the territory defined in the Declaration and can only be bottled out of this territory when provisions set forth by [Norma Oficial Mexicana] are met." Within these requirements about ingredients, however, there is a broad range of options when it comes to choosing a tequila, and knowing how to read a tequila bottle's label will help you choose the tequila that is best for you.

WHAT'S REALLY IMPORTANT

One basic choice facing tequila drinkers has to do with type. As we've discussed, there are five: blanco, also often called silver, is typically clear and unaged; joven is the product of blending blanco tequila with aged tequila; reposado is allowed to rest in

A HEART-TO-HEART ON THE DIFFERENCE BETWEEN MEZCAL AND TEQUILA

Though all tequilas are a subset of mezcals, there are several important differences that set tequilas apart. For instance, most mezcals are only distilled once, but tequila is distilled twice. One of the biggest differences has to do with processing the agave's heart, or piña. While the blue agave piñas used in tequila are cooked in steam ovens or autoclaves, those used in non-tequila mezcals are often cooked over charcoal in conical, rock-lined pit ovens known as *palenques*, which imparts on mezcals a smoky flavor absent from tequila.

oak barrels for two months to a year; añejo is aged in barrels for a year or longer; and extra añejo is aged for at least three years.

Another possible consideration is blue agave content, which ranges from 51 percent at the lower end all the way to 100 percent. In general, the greater the blue agave content, the higher the price. During a blue agave shortage in the late 1990s—caused by a rare frost in 1996 and the Fusarium blight (caused by the spread of a fungi known as *Fusarium roseum*) that killed more than one quarter of Mexico's agave crop—some distilleries stopped production of 100 percent blue agave tequila in order to keep tastes down for consumers.

LABEL LEGALESE

Another element to look for on a tequila label is the four-digit NOM number, which is issued to manufacturers in a broad range of industries. A NOM number on tequila bottles both confirms that the tequila was distilled and bottled in Mexico and identifies the distillery that produced it. Some brands share a NOM number, which indicates that those brands are both produced by the same distillery; currently there are approximately just over one hundred distillers producing about one thousand brands of tequila. Labels must also include the distiller's name and town of operation. However, this can be confusing, because some brands do not even have a distillery, instead purchasing large quantities of various distilleries' tequila and packaging under a well-known brand name (such as Patrón). In addition, some distillers lease out their land or facilities to other tequila companies to cultivate their own crop of blue agave or distill a small batch of tequila. In fact, many so-called "premium" tequila distillers operate this way.

In addition to the NOM number, the CRT requires that tequila labels include its endorsement that the contents meet the CRT's standards for being called tequila. Tequila labels must also include a list of any additives and a lot or batch code. Finally, tequila must have "hecho en Mexico" ("made in Mexico") printed on the label or the bottle.

TRUTH IN ADVERTISING

The Consejo Regulador del Tequila (CRT) prohibits distillers from printing on their labels accurate but misleading statements—like "100% Mexican" or "100% agave"—that might confuse consumers about the tequila's blue agave content. Generally, tequila aficionados are most interested in blue agave content, prizing it over other factors (like age). That being said, this content is not the same thing as quality.

QUALITY CONTROL

All of this might seem like overkill, but the purpose is to control quality and help consumers distinguish between authentic and fake tequila, which is a serious problem: In the eighteen years between 2002 and 2020, governments around the world intercepted and destroyed 3.5 million liters of fake tequila. In October 2020 alone, Mexico's government destroyed just under 200,000 liters of fake tequila that, had it been allowed to reach the market, would have cost the government more than Mex$18.5 million. Not for nothing, Dr. Dirk Lachenmeier of Germany's Chemical and Veterinary Investigation Agency described tequila as "one of the best regulated spirits in the world with strict . . . standards and labeling regulations."

❋ ❋ ❋

TASTING
TEQUILA

CHOOSING A TEQUILA

Although tequila is produced from only a single variety of agave that is grown in a relatively small geographic area, its flavors can vary widely. Soil, topography, and climate combine to give tequilas *terroir*, or a characteristic taste imparted by the environment in which the agave was grown. For instance, tequilas made from blue agave grown in the highlands of central Jalisco tend to be fruitier when compared to those produced from agaves grown in the region's lowlands. As a result, tequilas can take on everything from notes of honey (from high ash soils) to coconut (rocky areas) to clove (salty soils).

In addition, aging plays a critical role in tequila's taste. Blanco, or unaged tequila, tends to have a more distinctive agave flavor and is therefore harsher or rougher than the mellowed flavors

of either reposado or añejo tequilas. Naturally, the longer the tequila is aged, the more of the oak's flavor and color it takes on, sometimes overpowering the agave. For this reason, many tequila enthusiasts will avoid añejo tequilas, preferring either reposados or blancos. Even the type of oak used in the barrels plays a role, with American oak barrels producing notes of vanilla, French oak leaving behind traces of fruit, and bourbon barrels imparting a distinctive caramel flavor.

Higher-quality tequilas are almost always packaged in airtight bottles because oxidation—the process by which oxygen changes a liquid's chemical makeup—weakens the tequila's flavor and aroma. While a sealed bottle of tequila will last for years, once the bottle is opened you have about two months to consume it before

HANGOVERS

Tequila has a reputation for inspiring bad behavior. As tech guru Mitch Ratcliffe once noted, "A computer lets you make more mistakes faster than any other invention with the possible exceptions of handguns and Tequila." In addition to bad decisions, there's the dreadful hangover. In a 2017 survey on addictions.com, 22.9 percent of respondents claimed that tequila produced the worst hangovers. This is ironic because blanco tequilas contain none of the sugars that contribute to the not-feeling-so-good mornings after. Reposado and añejo tequilas absorb some of these hangover-causing elements while aging in barrels. Therefore, for a night of heavy drinking, reach for the 100 percent agave blanco tequila; you'll thank me in the morning!

oxidation ruins the tequila. According to some experts, within three to six months, opened tequila begins tasting like bourbon, having lost the distinctive agave flavor.

BEFORE YOU POUR

Make sure to carefully peruse the label, looking for clues as to what to expect. Is this a blanco? A reposado? An añejo? Understanding those terms and their flavor profiles will help prepare you to fully appreciate the tequila's distinctive flavor and aromas. Color is another important consideration. Blanco is clear because it has not been aged in barrels (liquor that has been aged absorbs the barrels' coloring, taking on a brown hue). Tequila with a brown hue has sometimes been aged in oak barrels, which means, in addition to a mellowed agave flavor, you will often get an oaky taste caused by the tannins in the wood. Pay attention, though: Some distillers color their blanco tequilas by mixing it with either aged tequilas or colorants and sweeteners designed to soften the alcohol's taste, producing joven or gold tequilas.

SERVING

It is important to remember
that tequila is designed to be
drunk straight, rather than in
cocktails. Tequila cocktails
started as a way of covering
the taste of low-quality
tequila (although a well-
crafted cocktail sometimes
accentuates and harmonizes
with tequila's natural flavors).
In Mexico, most tequila is
served straight (also known
as neat, both of which mean
no ice or chilling) and sipped
rather than drunk as a shot.

Sometimes the tequila will be served with a chaser, such as
sangrita, or "little blood" (chili powder mixed with orange and
tomato juices). By contrast, in the United States, tequila is often
consumed mixed in a cocktail (like a margarita) or taken as a
shot, along with salt and a lime or lemon wedge. The practice
of quickly gulping tequila and chasing it with bitter chasers
goes back at least a century, and likely grew out of the fact that
the tequila available to Americans at the time was generally
low quality and therefore tasted bad (a characteristic of cheap
tequilas or of tequilas that have spoiled due to oxidation).
Tequila connoisseurs sip their tequila straight to fully enjoy the
unique tastes and aromas that each brand has to offer.

If you are not drinking tequila as part of a cocktail and
want to fully appreciate its taste, the best way to serve it is at
room temperature. Because true connoisseurs pay attention to

"IS THERE A DOCTOR IN THE HOUSE?"

In college, I used to joke that I was majoring in beer. People laughed, but the joke's on me: Now you actually can get a degree in tequila! San Francisco's famed Tommy's Mexican Restaurant, which opened in 1965, offers courses in tequila as part of its "Blue Agave Club." Patrons can earn a "Master's" degree in tequila by drinking thirty-five different types of tequila over twelve or more visits to the bar. Having achieved that feat, they receive a diploma and a T-shirt announcing their achievement to the world. Feel like going for the brass ring? Tasting an additional thirty-five types of tequila and answering a "notoriously difficult" final exam will earn you either a PhD (if the tequila was in mixed drinks) or the designation "Ninja Master" (if you drank your tequila neat). Want to go even further? Visit a tequila distillery in Mexico after earning your tequila PhD or Ninja Master designation and Tommy's will declare you a "Demigod of Tequila!" At about $500 for the cost of the tequila, it is one of the lowest-priced graduate degrees around. Just don't expect your mom to start calling you "Doctor."

the tequila's color, they prefer clear glassware. There is no "official" tequila glass; a clear cognac, wine, or Glencairn glass, or a champagne flute, will suffice. These trap the tequila's aromas to help accentuate the taste. Once you have poured the tequila into your glass, place it over a white surface to fully appreciate its color. It is also recommended to slowly turn it side to side so the tequila creeps up the glass's side; as it settles, you can fully appreciate the tequila's color.

NOSE BEFORE YOU SIP

Because of the variety of flavors and aromas in blue agave and the different methods of distilling tequila, you will want to pay particular attention to its "nose," or aroma. Before tasting, bring the glass to your nose. Inhale slowly and gently, noting the absence or presence of sweetness, the astringency of the alcohol, and the presence of any other aromas. Next, swirl the tequila gently in the glass and then take another sniff. Swirling the tequila helps awaken its full aromas and can bring to the surface subtle notes you may have missed the first time around. You may detect

SWEET
brown sugar
butterscotch
caramel/toffee
chocolate
gingerbread
honey
maple syrup
molasses

FRUITY
apple
berry
cherry
coconut
dark fruit
grapefruit
lemon
lime
peach
pineapple

WOODY AND NUTTY
almond
char
coffee
oak
roasted nuts
smoke

VEGETAL AND SPICY
anise
asparagus
black pepper
celery
cinnamon
clove
dill
gardenia
geranium
grass
jasmine
lavender
menthol
nutmeg

pepper
rose
rosemary
tea
thyme
tobacco

PUNGENT
burnt match
gasoline
skunk
wet wool
whiskey

SIPPING

After you've appreciated the complexity of the aroma, sip a small amount of the tequila, letting it rest on your tongue for about twenty seconds. Next, swirl it around your mouth (different areas of your tongue detect different tastes, so something as complex as tequila requires use of the whole tongue). Now swallow, but before moving on to the next sip, try to identify what, if any, tastes linger. Did the flavors in the aroma carry over to the taste? One tip is to sniff coffee beans between tastes; doing so resets your nasal passages, in effect cleansing your palate and reducing tasting fatigue. Doing this will help ensure you are as sharp for your second taste as you were for your first.

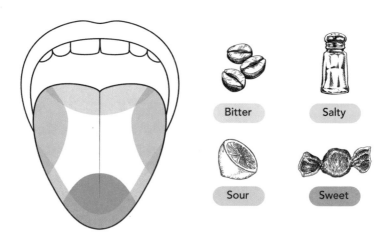

Bitter   Salty

Sour   Sweet

DON'T DRIVE YOUR DRINK

We all know tequila can power a good time but did you know it can also power a car? It's true! In 1963, Chrysler developed a car powered by the A1 turbine engine that could run on alcohol. Since the 1930s, Chrysler had experimented with turbine engines, which had longer operational lives, and fewer parts and were lighter than traditional piston engines. Between October 1963 and January 1966, Chrysler let 203 drivers test fifty-five cars with the turbine engines, typically using diesel fuel, kerosene, or standard unleaded fuel. However, in one particularly notable instance, Mexican President Adolfo Mateos (1958–1964) rode in the car on a test drive fueled by a few gallons of tequila! Unfortunately, the cars were simply a test for Chrysler's long-running turbine engine program and never entered production. Of the fifty-five test vehicles, most were destroyed. Of the remaining cars, most are in museums, though late night talk show host Jay Leno, a noted car collector, owns one of them. There's no word on whether he's ever fueled it with tequila.

THE FINISH

Tequila is a complicated spirit with lots of moving parts, so paying attention to the finish is very important; lots of key flavors only make themselves apparent on the back end. Also notice how your mouth feels. What is the body like? Is it creamy or thick? Maybe smooth and light? Does it leave your mouth feeling dry or burnt? Has any particular flavor lingered or changed? Make sure to take note of these in your journal as they point to the unique preparation and agave that make up the particular tequila you were tasting.

THE OTHER GUYS

While tequila is the best-known Mexican spirit, it is far from the only one. There are of course all the other forms of mezcal. In addition, there is sotol, a liquor distilled from the dasylirion, or desert spoon plant, which grows in the Chihuahuan Desert (spanning northern Mexico and a portion of the southwestern United States).

Mexico granted sotol an appellation of origin in 2002 that restricts its manufacture to the states of Chihuahua, Coahuila, and Durango, though some US producers also distill it. In addition, several types of agave can also be distilled to produce *raicilla* ("little root"), a 100 proof liquor that is more floral than tequila. Raicilla is produced in two categories—de la costa ("costal") and de la sierra ("mountainous")—based on where in Jalisco the agaves used were grown.

TASTING A FLIGHT

If you're tasting a flight of tequilas, try to make sure the selection features diverse styles, such as a blanco, reposado, and añejo, perhaps all from the same brand. It's a good idea to go from the lightest to the darkest, because if you go for the more intense flavors first, you could blow out your taste buds. Go slow. Enjoy yourself. There's no need to rush through the flight. Spend time with each tequila and take a break in between to give your palate time to reset.

Another way to do it is to taste a blind flight, where the spirit is poured for you and you don't know the brand or age of the tequila you're tasting. This way you can experience the taste without any preconceptions. If you're doing a side-by-side comparison of the same type by two brands and don't want to let too much time pass between tasting each sample, be sure to use a palate cleanser as you switch back and forth.

* * *

FAMOUS
TEQUILAS

NAMES YOU KNOW

There is, of course, near endless debate over which tequilas are the best, which expensive bottles are worth their price, and whether or not some of the most popular brands are overrated. You'll have to form your own opinions about those issues. What's presented here is a shortlist of some nice bottles that range from the eminently affordable to the special occasional (read: expensive). This collection will teach you a lot about what you like and don't like, and what's worth and not worth the price, when you're first starting to take tasting seriously. While your personal go-to favorite might not be listed here, that just means you can start there with your own tasting notes on the journal pages that follow.

1800 TEQUILA
1800 SILVER

ABV:
40% (80 PROOF)
NOM 1122

1800 bills itself as "the best taste in tequila" and takes its name from the first year in which tequila that had been aged in wood barrels was sold. Started as a brand of the Jose Cuervo company in 1975 as a premium sipping brand, in 2004, the company launched silver, reposado, and añejo varieties, all of which are 100 percent blue agave tequilas. Four years later, the company introduced what it called "Select Silver," the first 100 proof blanco tequila.

1800's Silver is among the company's best-known and popular brands. The packaging is sleek, minimalist, and modern, featuring a clear glass bottle and small blue-and-white labels. Produced in the Los Valles region of north central Jalisco, Silver is produced from 100 percent blue agave that is cooked in an autoclave and fermented in stainless steel tanks. The final product is 80 proof and is considered a moderately priced tequila. It gives off a strong agave aroma; this characterizes the taste as well, which is not surprising given that the Silver is not aged at all. Sippers will also note a strong taste and smell of alcohol followed by a similarly strong peppery flavor that is common to blue agave. Frequently, people will also notice notes of citrus in both the aroma and the taste. It is generally considered a solid tequila that can be enjoyed both on its own and mixed in a cocktail.

CALLE 23
AÑEJO

ABV:
40% (80 PROOF)
NOM 1545

Calle 23 is a whimsical tequila distillery (slogan "agave you my heart") started in the early 2000s by a French biological chemist named Sophie Decobecq. During a 1999 visit to Mexico, Decobecq fell in love with both the country and tequila, and she permanently relocated in 2003. Calle 23 is located in the Los Altos region of Jalisco, which is the highlands. According to Calle 23, this location produces unusually high-quality blue agave, which gives the company's tequilas their distinctive taste. Controversially, Decobecq cooks all of the company's blue agave in an autoclave because it gives her greater control over the process. Calle 23 then uses local well water in the company's bagasse bed and ferments the aguamiel in open-air, stainless-steel tanks. Decobecq has traveled extensively through the region collecting yeast samples and uses two: a strain for blanco and añejo and another for reposado. The use of two different yeast strains sets Calle 23 apart from most other tequila manufacturers. All varieties of Calle 23 tequilas are bottled similarly, the only difference being the labels' colors (red for blanco, black for reposado, and gold for añejo).

Both the reposado and the añejo are aged in American white oak barrels (eight and sixteen months, respectively). This process creates a full-bodied añejo that has a dark amber color. The resulting tequila has a medium vanilla flavor and smell that, coupled with a caramel aftertaste, does not diminish or mask the agave. Calle 23's añejo is moderately priced and intended to be sipped straight, though the company's website does include several cocktail suggestions.

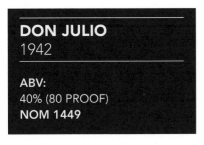

DON JULIO
1942

ABV:
40% (80 PROOF)
NOM 1449

Don Julio 1942 is a special issue añejo that celebrates the year that the company was founded. In 1942, seventeen-year-old Don Julio González-Frausto Estrada began distilling tequila, later establishing his own distillery, La Primavera ("the springtime"), in Atotonilco El Alto ("place of the hot waters" and "the high one"), a town in west central Jalisco. Don Julio's reputation for quality spread quickly, and sales of its tequila took off, though the first bottle to bear the name "Don Julio" did not appear until 1985 (up to that time, the distillery's key brand was Tres Magueyes). Don Julio is currently the world's largest producer of tequila by volume even as other brands have greater name recognition in the United States and around the world.

1942 is a premium sipping tequila aged for at least thirty months. Don Julio harvests the blue agaves from the Los Altos region of Jalisco, cooks them in stone ovens, and ages the tequila in white oak bourbon barrels. The result is a very smooth sipping tequila with substantial vanilla, caramel, and oak notes. Some tasters even call it a "sweet" tequila, although it is not overly so; it just lacks the agave bite characteristic of blanco tequilas. At more than one hundred dollars per bottle, this is hardly an entry-level tequila.

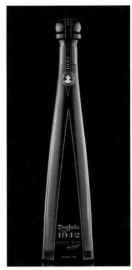

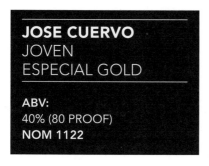

JOSE CUERVO
JOVEN
ESPECIAL GOLD

ABV:
40% (80 PROOF)
NOM 1122

Jose Cuervo is one of the first names that come to mind when people think of tequila, and the Especial Gold is one of the company's most ubiquitous offerings. This is surely due in part to the fact that Jose Cuervo is Mexico's oldest and among its largest tequila distilleries, and the company introduced a number of innovations (such as bottling tequila for individual sale) that made it synonymous with tequila. During Prohibition, Jose Cuervo captured a significant share of the US market for tequila and that presence only grew during World War II, when the US imposed restrictions on European imports and many American distilleries converted to producing wartime necessities. Currently, Jose Cuervo supplies about one-third of the US market for tequila.

Jose Cuervo tequila is produced at the Fábrica La Rojeña distillery just an hour outside Guadalajara (Mexico's second-largest city) in the center of Jalisco. The company uses a wide variety of blue agave from all over Jalisco to produce Especial Gold and, rather than cooking the agaves in an oven, heats them using water in a process called acid-thermal hydrolysis. The inulin is then extracted using a diffuser and fermented in stainless steel tanks. Unlike the other tequilas on this list, Especial Gold is only 51 percent agave, with other sugars

and caramel coloring added during the manufacturing process, making it a mixto tequila. In addition, Jose Cuervo combines blanco and reposado tequilas to create a joven with a consistent feel and taste for the Especial Gold across batches.

On the one hand, this creates an inexpensive product, which surely helps account for Jose Cuervo's popularity, name recognition, and large share of US tequila sales. On the other hand, Especial Gold is harsher than either reposado or añejo offerings. The primary aroma and taste is alcohol followed closely by cooked agave. In a tasting, tequila drinkers also noted the tastes of astringent, salt, and pepper. Often, Jose Cuervo is used for cocktails rather than sipped, which helps mellow some of the tequila's harsher features.

PATRÓN SPIRITS COMPANY
EXTRA AÑEJO
10 AÑOS

ABV:
40% (80 PROOF)
NOM 1492

Another well-known tequila brand is Patrón, which styles itself as an "ultra-premium" brand. Originally produced by 7 Leguas Tequila (founded in 1952 by Ignacio González Vargas), in 1989 the Patrón brand was purchased by St. Maarten Spirits, Ltd. In 2018, St. Maarten Spirits, Ltd sold the Patrón brand to Bacardi Limited, which owns a slew of well-known brands, including Dewar's scotch, Grey Goose vodka, Bombay Sapphire gin, and (of course) Bacardí rum.

Patrón is thoroughly "old-school" when it comes to distilling tequila, using 100 percent blue agave, baking the piñas in small brick ovens and crushing them using a stone tahona mill. Next, Patrón distills the aguamiel for three days. For the Patrón Extra

Añejo 10 Años, which is part of Patrón's "Limited Edition" collection, this means fermentation in wood tanks, often with agave fibers, which some distillers believe increases the agave taste. The resulting tequila is then aged for ten years in white oak barrels before (like all Patrón tequilas) being sealed in glass bottles by a cork topped with a crystal stopper. Naturally, these extra flourishes come at a cost: a 750 mL bottle of Patrón Extra Añejo 10 Años will set you back about $400 in the United States.

However, many enthusiasts believe the cost is more than worth it. The resulting tequila presents with very subtle caramel, fruit, and vanilla flavors and aromas, with tasters mentioning a dried fruit taste reminiscent of cherries or apricots. The agave flavor is quite mild (in some cases almost undetectable) with none of the bite common to younger tequilas.

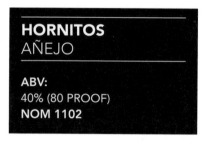

HORNITOS
AÑEJO

ABV:
40% (80 PROOF)
NOM 1102

Hornitos is a brand familiar to many casual tequila drinkers. The tequila Hornitos Reposado is a bargain brand from a distillery established in 1950 by Don Francisco Javier Sauza, an offshoot of the larger Sauza Tequila company founded in 1873 that he had taken over in 1931. Since 1988, Sauza and its brands (including Sauza and Hornitos) have been owned and produced by Pedro Domecq, S.A. Interestingly, Don Francisco was one of the leading forces behind Mexico's declaration that "true" tequila could only be produced in Mexico.

That commitment to quality and national history is visible in Hornitos Reposado tequila. Don Francisco started the Hornitos brand to celebrate Mexican independence, and the reposado is made with 100 percent blue agave. However, unlike premium brands, Hornitos cooks the piñas in an autoclave, extracts the aguamiel using a diffuser, and ferments the tequila in stainless steel tanks. In the case of the brand's blanco tequila, Hornitos Plata, this often leaves a harsh chemical taste, but the little bit of aging softens that in the añejo. What's left is strong aromas of wood, chocolate, and fruit and a slightly sweet taste that carries over the aroma but also agave and alcohol that leave a dry finish.

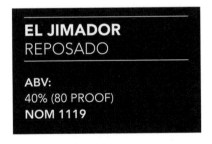

EL JIMADOR
REPOSADO

ABV:
40% (80 PROOF)
NOM 1119

The brand el Jimador takes its name from the workers who harvest the agave plants used in mezcals. The brand is owned by Brown-Forman, an American liquor conglomerate founded in 1870 by a pharmaceuticals salesman named George Garvin Brown in Louisville, Kentucky. In 1994, Brown-Forman launched el Jimador, which bills itself as "the world's first premium tequila at an accessible price point." El Jimador's tequilas are made with 100 percent blue agave harvested from Casa Herradura, which is located in Amatitán in western Jalisco. Casa Herradura supplies other brands with agaves as well, including its own Tequila Herradura.

Being budget conscious means that el Jimador cooks its blue agave using acid-thermal hydrolysis and extracts the aguamiel with a diffuser. El Jimador is then fermented in stainless steel tanks. As a result, the blanco tends to have an overwhelming aroma and taste of agave, alcohol, and pepper that is frequently described as "medicinal." The reposado's aging softens those flavors and aromas quite a bit, softening but not eliminating the agave and alcohol taste while adding notes of oak and vanilla. However, some tasters note a harsh aftertaste, though that is by no means a universal sentiment. In general, this tequila occupies a middle ground between mixing and sipping, an indication perhaps of the difficulty of creating a premium taste at a bargain price.

TEQUILA CORRALEJO
REPOSADO

ABV:
40% (80 PROOF)
NOM 1119

In 2021, *Luxe Digital* named Tequila Corralejo's reposado the best value tequila, an assessment echoed by *Forbes*. Hacienda Corralejo is located in the town of Abasolo in the state of Guanajuato, on the very edge of Mexico's tequila-producing region. Founded in 1755, the distillery is one of Mexico's oldest and claims to be the country's oldest commercial distillery. Though Hacienda Corralejo has been around for more than two centuries, it makes use of a mix of ancient and modern distilling methods. On the one hand, it cooks its 100 percent blue agave piñas in autoclaves but then crushes them using an old-school roller mill before fermenting the aguamiel in stainless steel tanks.

Interestingly, the mosto is then distilled in a Charentais still (the type used to produce cognac) before being aged in barrels made from a combination of American, French, and Mexican oak.

The resulting tequila, which generally runs under thirty dollars per bottle, has the distinctive cooked agave and alcohol aromas and flavors as well as pronounced notes of pepper. However, unlike most value tequilas, there are also substantial undertones of vanilla and smoke, though many consumers may find these difficult to discern. Like most of Tequila Corralejo's products, the reposado comes packaged in distinctive elongated bottles (this one sapphire blue), which makes it stand out on any shelf.

HERRADURA
SILVER

ABV:
40% (80 PROOF)
NOM 1119

Grupo Industrial Herradura is a subsidiary of the US liquor conglomerate Brown-Forman. The company not only produces its own tequila (under the Herradura label), but it also supplies blue agave to several other tequila distilleries, a mark of its quality (it has a reputation for being the best for producing tequila). Tequila production at Herradura stretched back to the early nineteenth century, though it was in 1870, when

Félix López took over the distillery and blue agave cultivation that things really took off. López expanded agave cultivation and tequila production by improving the facilities, and after his death in 1878, his widow, Carmen, continued to grow the business. The arrival of railroads helped the company, which remained within the family until 2007, though in the 1960s production started at a newer, larger facility (the old one was operated as a historic site and museum).

Herradura's Blanco 46, which costs approximately $400 per 750 mL bottle, is undoubtedly one of the company's premium brands, but it's not the easiest to find. More well known, especially in the US, is Herradura Silver. Aged in white oak barrels, this tequila has a light straw color to it, and while it has some of the wood barrel in its aroma, what you really smell is strong notes of agave, citrus, and vanilla. Sweet but peppery, you taste plenty of agave and fruit when you sip it.

CASAMIGOS TEQUILA
REPOSADO

ABV:
40% (80 PROOF)
NOM 1609

I know what you are thinking: George Clooney's tequila? How can a celebrity tequila possibly be any good? After all, isn't it just trading on Clooney's name? The answer is "Yes, but . . ." Founded in 2013 by Clooney and his partners, entrepreneur Rande Gerber and property developer Mike Meldman, as an "ultra-premium, small-batch" tequila brand, Casamigos had all of the makings of a marketing stunt. However, despite expectations, Casamigos is actually pretty good, and in any event Clooney, Gerber, and Meldman sold the company in 2017 to British beverage company Diageo (though Clooney's face is still prominent on the Casamigos website and his signature appears on the bottle).

One reason for Casamigos's quality and popularity is the process: It is made from 100 percent blue agave piñas cooked in brick ovens for seventy-two hours. The cooked piñas are then crushed in a tahona and the aguamiel is fermented in steel tanks for eighty hours (nearly double the usual forty-eight) using what Casamigos describes as a "proprietary blend" of yeast. The company rests the blanco for two months, the reposado for seven months, and the añejo for fourteen, all in American white oak barrels. The resulting aroma and flavor profile of the reposado are quite different from those of almost all the other bottles in this chapter. The most distinctive flavor is vanilla, which is incredibly strong and balanced by a slightly weaker caramel taste. Lurking behind these are notes of agave and oak but also, surprisingly, butter, butterscotch, and cinnamon. These are softened considerably in the añejo, which is more closely balanced between the dominant caramel and vanilla flavors and the notes of agave and oak. In both cases, the taste of alcohol is nearly invisible, a testament to the high quality of the blue agave that Casamigos uses and the company's workmanlike approach to distillation. Most surprising is that, despite Casamigos's "ultra-premium" pretensions, the cost of a 750 mL bottle of Casamigos Tequila Reposado will set you back only about fifty dollars, far less than other brands.

* * *

TEQUILA
COCKTAILS

PALOMA

The paloma is a true Mexican tequila cocktail, so it is only fitting that it would be included in this book. The cocktail's origins are somewhat murky, however, with most scholars having concluded that it emerged during the 1950s. The cocktail is a light, effervescent, and refreshing drink that makes use of fruit flavors to elevate the tequila's natural taste. You definitely want to stick to either blanco (preferred) or reposado tequila for this one because the oak flavoring that accompanies aging clashes with the paloma's fruit flavors.

2 ounces tequila
½ ounce freshly squeezed lime
 juice
grapefruit soda to top (can
 substitute freshly squeezed
 grapefruit juice and club soda)

1 lime wedge
coarse salt (optional)

Rub the lime wedge along a highball glass's rim and then dip the glass in salt if desired. Add the tequila to the glass followed by the lime juice. Top off the glass with the grapefruit soda and garnish with the lime wedge.

MARGARITA

Most Americans' introduction to tequila comes from the margarita (Spanish for "daisy"), which can be prepared in a variety of different ways. This recipe was one of the earliest published in the United States and would have been how most Americans first experienced what quickly became a popular drink across the country. (See page 17 for more on the margarita's history.)

1 ounce tequila
1 tablespoon freshly squeezed lime juice (about ½ a lime, or you can use lemon)

1 dash of triple sec
1 lime wedge
coarse salt

Pour the tequila, lime juice, and triple sec into a shaker of ice and shake vigorously until the shaker is almost too cold to hold. Circle a margarita glass's rim with the lime wedge, and spin the rim in the salt. Strain the shaker's contents into the glass and serve. (Rocks are optional.)

VARIATION

As an alternative, you can make what is called a Tommy's margarita, after San Francisco's well-known Tommy's Mexican Restaurant. In this version, substitute a shot of agave nectar for the triple sec.

TEXAS RANCH WATER

Given that Texas was once a part of Mexico (we don't talk about that; it was a messy breakup), it should come as no surprise that Texans love their tequila, and no tequila recipe book would be complete without this well-known and simple cocktail. Texas ranch water has been called the unofficial cocktail of western Texas, and there are all sorts of wild stories about its concoction. One is that a half-crazed rancher living in Fort Davis, Texas, came up with the cocktail during the 1960s. Whatever the true story is, I think you'll agree this is a delicious way to enjoy your tequila that's simple to prepare. Just as with the paloma, you'll want to stick with blanco or (if you have to) reposado tequila, and for the same reason: this is a light cocktail and the oak flavor that accompanies aging will weigh it down.

3 ounces tequila
1½ ounces freshly squeezed lime juice

Topo Chico mineral water (in a pinch you can substitute club soda)
1 lime wedge

Fill a highball glass with ice. Pour in the tequila, followed by the lime juice. Top off with the Topo Chico and garnish with a lime wedge.

TEQUILA SUNRISE

The tequila sunrise is one of the best-known tequila-based cocktails out there, due in no small measure to the title of the hit 1988 movie starring Mel Gibson, Michelle Pfeiffer, and Kurt Russell. The cocktail was invented in the 1930s but bears little resemblance to the drink as it's understood today, having been heavily modified in the 1970s. The version below is the "official" cocktail recipe, as defined by the International Bartenders Association.

1½ ounces tequila
¾ cup freshly squeezed orange juice

¾ ounce grenadine syrup
1 maraschino cherry
1 orange slice

Fill a highball glass with ice. Pour in the tequila followed by the orange juice. Drizzle in the grenadine syrup by pouring it over the back of a spoon poised over the highball glass. Add the maraschino cherry and garnish with the orange slice.

LONG ISLAND ICED TEA

The Long Island iced tea is not exactly a tequila cocktail because it includes several forms of liquor. Nevertheless, there's tequila in there and every bartender in the world knows how to make one. Like most cocktails, the origins of the Long Island iced tea are hard to pin down, though the best-known story is that bartender Robert "Rosebud" Butt invented the drink in 1972 while working at Long Island's Oak Beach Inn (in later years, his car's vanity plate read "LI ICET"). This is among the most complicated cocktails described in this book due to the sheer quantity and variety of ingredients.

½ ounce tequila
½ ounce vodka
½ ounce white rum
½ ounce triple sec
½ ounce gin

1 ounce freshly squeezed
   lemon juice
1 ounce simple syrup
splash of cola
1 lemon slice

Fill a tall glass with ice. Add the tequila, vodka, white rum, triple sec, gin, lemon juice, and simple syrup. Top off with a splash of cola, then stir and garnish with a lemon slice.

TASTING NOTES

ENJOYING TEQUILA

TEQUILA
The Details

Brand Name		Distiller	
Age	ABV/Proof		Date
Distiller's Location	Price per Glass/Bottle		Tasting Location

NOSE
Choose All That Apply

SWEET
- ○ brown sugar
- ○ butterscotch
- ○ caramel/toffee
- ○ chocolate
- ○ gingerbread
- ○ honey
- ○ maple syrup
- ○ molasses

FRUITY
- ○ apple

- ○ berry
- ○ cherry
- ○ coconut
- ○ dark fruit
- ○ grapefruit
- ○ lemon
- ○ lime
- ○ peach
- ○ pineapple

WOODY & NUTTY
- ○ almond

- ○ char
- ○ coffee
- ○ oak
- ○ roasted nuts
- ○ smoke

VEGETAL & SPICY
- ○ anise
- ○ asparagus
- ○ black pepper
- ○ cinnamon
- ○ clove

- ○ dill
- ○ gardenia
- ○ geranium
- ○ grass
- ○ jasmine
- ○ lavender
- ○ menthol
- ○ nutmeg
- ○ pepper
- ○ rose
- ○ rosemary

- ○ tea
- ○ thyme
- ○ tobacco

PUNGENT
- ○ burnt match
- ○ gasoline
- ○ skunk
- ○ wet wool
- ○ whiskey

OTHER
....

STYLE
Choose One

- ○ Neat
- ○ With Water
- ○ Cocktail

COLOR
Circle One

TASTING WHEEL

Rate your tasting experience, 1 (lowest) to 5 (highest)

Linger, Legs, Body, Finish, Balance, Bite, Sweet, Pungency, Citrusy, Herbal, Spicy, Floral, Earthy, Smoky, Woody, Nutty

TASTING NOTES

Describe the First Sip

....

....

....

Describe the Third Sip

....

....

....

Describe the Body and Finish

....

....

....

What Is Most Striking About This Tequila?

....

....

....

Additional Notes

....

....

....

....

GUIDED TASTING

Write It Out

QUALITY RATING

☆ ☆ ☆ ☆ ☆

COST RATING

OVERALL RATING

RATE IT

Fill It In

TEQUILA
The Details

Brand Name

Distiller

Age

ABV/Proof

Date

Distiller's Location

Price per Glass/Bottle

Tasting Location

NOSE
Choose All That Apply

SWEET
- ○ brown sugar
- ○ butterscotch
- ○ caramel/toffee
- ○ chocolate
- ○ gingerbread
- ○ honey
- ○ maple syrup
- ○ molasses

FRUITY
- ○ apple

- ○ berry
- ○ cherry
- ○ coconut
- ○ dark fruit
- ○ grapefruit
- ○ lemon
- ○ lime
- ○ peach
- ○ pineapple

WOODY & NUTTY
- ○ almond

- ○ char
- ○ coffee
- ○ oak
- ○ roasted nuts
- ○ smoke

VEGETAL & SPICY
- ○ anise
- ○ asparagus
- ○ black pepper
- ○ cinnamon
- ○ clove

- ○ dill
- ○ gardenia
- ○ geranium
- ○ grass
- ○ jasmine
- ○ lavender
- ○ menthol
- ○ nutmeg
- ○ pepper
- ○ rose
- ○ rosemary

- ○ tea
- ○ thyme
- ○ tobacco

PUNGENT
- ○ burnt match
- ○ gasoline
- ○ skunk
- ○ wet wool
- ○ whiskey

OTHER

STYLE
Choose One

- ○ Neat
- ○ With Water
- ○ Cocktail

COLOR
Circle One

TASTING WHEEL

Rate your tasting experience, 1 (lowest) to 5 (highest)

Legs · Body · Balance · Sweet · Citrusy · Spicy · Earthy · Nutty · Woody · Smoky · Floral · Herbal · Pungency · Bite · Finish · Linger

TASTING NOTES

Describe the First Sip

....

....

....

Describe the Third Sip

....

....

....

Describe the Body and Finish

....

....

....

What Is Most Striking About This Tequila?

....

....

....

Additional Notes

....

....

....

....

QUALITY RATING	COST RATING	OVERALL RATING
☆ ☆ ☆ ☆ ☆	ⓢ ⓢ ⓢ ⓢ ⓢ	

TEQUILA
The Details

Brand Name

Distiller

Age

ABV/Proof

Date

Distiller's Location

Price per Glass/Bottle

Tasting Location

NOSE
Choose All That Apply

SWEET
- ○ brown sugar
- ○ butterscotch
- ○ caramel/toffee
- ○ chocolate
- ○ gingerbread
- ○ honey
- ○ maple syrup
- ○ molasses

FRUITY
- ○ apple

- ○ berry
- ○ cherry
- ○ coconut
- ○ dark fruit
- ○ grapefruit
- ○ lemon
- ○ lime
- ○ peach
- ○ pineapple

WOODY & NUTTY
- ○ almond

- ○ char
- ○ coffee
- ○ oak
- ○ roasted nuts
- ○ smoke

VEGETAL & SPICY
- ○ anise
- ○ asparagus
- ○ black pepper
- ○ cinnamon
- ○ clove

- ○ dill
- ○ gardenia
- ○ geranium
- ○ grass
- ○ jasmine
- ○ lavender
- ○ menthol
- ○ nutmeg
- ○ pepper
- ○ rose
- ○ rosemary

- ○ tea
- ○ thyme
- ○ tobacco

PUNGENT
- ○ burnt match
- ○ gasoline
- ○ skunk
- ○ wet wool
- ○ whiskey

OTHER

STYLE
Choose One

- ○ Neat
- ○ With Water
- ○ Cocktail

COLOR
Circle One

TASTING WHEEL

Rate your tasting experience, 1 (lowest) to 5 (highest)

Legs · Body · Balance · Sweet · Citrusy · Spicy · Earthy · Nutty · Woody · Smoky · Floral · Herbal · Pungency · Bite · Finish · Linger

TASTING NOTES

Describe the First Sip

....

....

....

Describe the Third Sip

....

....

....

Describe the Body and Finish

....

....

....

What Is Most Striking About This Tequila?

....

....

....

Additional Notes

....

....

....

....

QUALITY RATING	COST RATING	OVERALL RATING	
			RATE IT Fill It In

ENJOYING TEQUILA

TEQUILA
The Details

Brand Name   **Distiller**

Age   **ABV/Proof**   **Date**

Distiller's Location   **Price per Glass/Bottle**   **Tasting Location**

NOSE
Choose All That Apply

SWEET
- ○ brown sugar
- ○ butterscotch
- ○ caramel/toffee
- ○ chocolate
- ○ gingerbread
- ○ honey
- ○ maple syrup
- ○ molasses

FRUITY
- ○ apple

- ○ berry
- ○ cherry
- ○ coconut
- ○ dark fruit
- ○ grapefruit
- ○ lemon
- ○ lime
- ○ peach
- ○ pineapple

WOODY & NUTTY
- ○ almond

- ○ char
- ○ coffee
- ○ oak
- ○ roasted nuts
- ○ smoke

VEGETAL & SPICY
- ○ anise
- ○ asparagus
- ○ black pepper
- ○ cinnamon
- ○ clove

- ○ dill
- ○ gardenia
- ○ geranium
- ○ grass
- ○ jasmine
- ○ lavender
- ○ menthol
- ○ nutmeg
- ○ pepper
- ○ rose
- ○ rosemary

- ○ tea
- ○ thyme
- ○ tobacco

PUNGENT
- ○ burnt match
- ○ gasoline
- ○ skunk
- ○ wet wool
- ○ whiskey

OTHER
....

STYLE
Choose One

- ○ Neat
- ○ With Water
- ○ Cocktail

COLOR
Circle One

TASTING WHEEL

Rate your tasting experience, 1 (lowest) to 5 (highest)

Legs, Body, Balance, Sweet, Citrusy, Spicy, Earthy, Nutty, Woody, Smoky, Floral, Herbal, Pungency, Bite, Finish, Linger

TASTING NOTES

Describe the First Sip

....

....

....

Describe the Third Sip

....

....

....

Describe the Body and Finish

....

....

....

What Is Most Striking About This Tequila?

....

....

....

Additional Notes

....

....

....

....

GUIDED TASTING

Write It Out

QUALITY RATING	COST RATING	OVERALL RATING

RATE IT

Fill It In

ENJOYING TEQUILA

TEQUILA — The Details

Brand Name

Distiller

Age

ABV/Proof

Date

Distiller's Location

Price per Glass/Bottle

Tasting Location

NOSE — Choose All That Apply

SWEET
- brown sugar
- butterscotch
- caramel/toffee
- chocolate
- gingerbread
- honey
- maple syrup
- molasses

FRUITY
- apple
- berry
- cherry
- coconut
- dark fruit
- grapefruit
- lemon
- lime
- peach
- pineapple

WOODY & NUTTY
- almond
- char
- coffee
- oak
- roasted nuts
- smoke

VEGETAL & SPICY
- anise
- asparagus
- black pepper
- cinnamon
- clove
- dill
- gardenia
- geranium
- grass
- jasmine
- lavender
- menthol
- nutmeg
- pepper
- rose
- rosemary
- tea
- thyme
- tobacco

PUNGENT
- burnt match
- gasoline
- skunk
- wet wool
- whiskey

OTHER
....

STYLE — Choose One

- Neat
- With Water
- Cocktail

COLOR — Circle One

TASTING WHEEL

Rate your tasting experience, 1 (lowest) to 5 (highest)

Legs, Body, Balance, Sweet, Citrusy, Spicy, Earthy, Nutty, Woody, Smoky, Floral, Herbal, Pungency, Bite, Finish, Linger

86

TASTING NOTES

Describe the First Sip

....

....

....

Describe the Third Sip

....

....

....

Describe the Body and Finish

....

....

....

What Is Most Striking About This Tequila?

....

....

....

Additional Notes

....

....

....

....

QUALITY RATING   **COST RATING**   **OVERALL RATING**

RATE IT

Fill It In

ENJOYING TEQUILA

TEQUILA
The Details

Brand Name

Distiller

Age

ABV/Proof

Date

Distiller's Location

Price per Glass/Bottle

Tasting Location

NOSE
Choose All That Apply

SWEET
- ◯ brown sugar
- ◯ butterscotch
- ◯ caramel/toffee
- ◯ chocolate
- ◯ gingerbread
- ◯ honey
- ◯ maple syrup
- ◯ molasses

FRUITY
- ◯ apple

- ◯ berry
- ◯ cherry
- ◯ coconut
- ◯ dark fruit
- ◯ grapefruit
- ◯ lemon
- ◯ lime
- ◯ peach
- ◯ pineapple

WOODY & NUTTY
- ◯ almond

- ◯ char
- ◯ coffee
- ◯ oak
- ◯ roasted nuts
- ◯ smoke

VEGETAL & SPICY
- ◯ anise
- ◯ asparagus
- ◯ black pepper
- ◯ cinnamon
- ◯ clove

- ◯ dill
- ◯ gardenia
- ◯ geranium
- ◯ grass
- ◯ jasmine
- ◯ lavender
- ◯ menthol
- ◯ nutmeg
- ◯ pepper
- ◯ rose
- ◯ rosemary

- ◯ tea
- ◯ thyme
- ◯ tobacco

PUNGENT
- ◯ burnt match
- ◯ gasoline
- ◯ skunk
- ◯ wet wool
- ◯ whiskey

OTHER
....

STYLE
Choose One

- ◯ Neat
- ◯ With Water
- ◯ Cocktail

COLOR
Circle One

TASTING WHEEL

Rate your tasting experience, 1 (lowest) to 5 (highest)

TASTING NOTES

Describe the First Sip

....

....

....

Describe the Third Sip

....

....

....

Describe the Body and Finish

....

....

....

What Is Most Striking About This Tequila?

....

....

....

Additional Notes

....

....

....

....

GUIDED TASTING

Write It Out

QUALITY RATING	COST RATING	OVERALL RATING
☆ ☆ ☆ ☆ ☆		

RATE IT

Fill It In

ENJOYING TEQUILA

TEQUILA — The Details

Brand Name   **Distiller**

Age   **ABV/Proof**   **Date**

Distiller's Location   **Price per Glass/Bottle**   **Tasting Location**

NOSE — Choose All That Apply

SWEET
- ◯ brown sugar
- ◯ butterscotch
- ◯ caramel/toffee
- ◯ chocolate
- ◯ gingerbread
- ◯ honey
- ◯ maple syrup
- ◯ molasses

FRUITY
- ◯ apple

- ◯ berry
- ◯ cherry
- ◯ coconut
- ◯ dark fruit
- ◯ grapefruit
- ◯ lemon
- ◯ lime
- ◯ peach
- ◯ pineapple

WOODY & NUTTY
- ◯ almond

- ◯ char
- ◯ coffee
- ◯ oak
- ◯ roasted nuts
- ◯ smoke

VEGETAL & SPICY
- ◯ anise
- ◯ asparagus
- ◯ black pepper
- ◯ cinnamon
- ◯ clove

- ◯ dill
- ◯ gardenia
- ◯ geranium
- ◯ grass
- ◯ jasmine
- ◯ lavender
- ◯ menthol
- ◯ nutmeg
- ◯ pepper
- ◯ rose
- ◯ rosemary

- ◯ tea
- ◯ thyme
- ◯ tobacco

PUNGENT
- ◯ burnt match
- ◯ gasoline
- ◯ skunk
- ◯ wet wool
- ◯ whiskey

OTHER

STYLE — Choose One

- ◯ Neat
- ◯ With Water
- ◯ Cocktail

TASTING WHEEL

Rate your tasting experience, 1 (lowest) to 5 (highest)

Legs, Body, Balance, Sweet, Citrusy, Spicy, Earthy, Nutty, Woody, Smoky, Floral, Herbal, Pungency, Bite, Finish, Linger

COLOR — Circle One

TASTING NOTES

Describe the First Sip

....

....

....

Describe the Third Sip

....

....

....

Describe the Body and Finish

....

....

....

What Is Most Striking About This Tequila?

....

....

....

Additional Notes

....

....

....

....

GUIDED TASTING

Write It Out

QUALITY RATING   **COST RATING**   **OVERALL RATING**

RATE IT

Fill It In

ENJOYING TEQUILA

TEQUILA
The Details

Brand Name

Distiller

Age

ABV/Proof

Date

Distiller's Location

Price per Glass/Bottle

Tasting Location

NOSE
Choose All That Apply

SWEET
- ○ brown sugar
- ○ butterscotch
- ○ caramel/toffee
- ○ chocolate
- ○ gingerbread
- ○ honey
- ○ maple syrup
- ○ molasses

FRUITY
- ○ apple

- ○ berry
- ○ cherry
- ○ coconut
- ○ dark fruit
- ○ grapefruit
- ○ lemon
- ○ lime
- ○ peach
- ○ pineapple

WOODY & NUTTY
- ○ almond

- ○ char
- ○ coffee
- ○ oak
- ○ roasted nuts
- ○ smoke

VEGETAL & SPICY
- ○ anise
- ○ asparagus
- ○ black pepper
- ○ cinnamon
- ○ clove

- ○ dill
- ○ gardenia
- ○ geranium
- ○ grass
- ○ jasmine
- ○ lavender
- ○ menthol
- ○ nutmeg
- ○ pepper
- ○ rose
- ○ rosemary

- ○ tea
- ○ thyme
- ○ tobacco

PUNGENT
- ○ burnt match
- ○ gasoline
- ○ skunk
- ○ wet wool
- ○ whiskey

OTHER

STYLE
Choose One

- ○ Neat
- ○ With Water
- ○ Cocktail

TASTING WHEEL
Rate your tasting experience, 1 (lowest) to 5 (highest)

Legs, Body, Balance, Sweet, Citrusy, Spicy, Earthy, Nutty, Woody, Smoky, Floral, Herbal, Pungency, Bite, Finish, Linger

COLOR
Circle One

TASTING NOTES

Describe the First Sip

....

....

....

Describe the Third Sip

....

....

....

Describe the Body and Finish

....

....

....

What Is Most Striking About This Tequila?

....

....

....

Additional Notes

....

....

....

....

GUIDED TASTING
Write It Out

QUALITY RATING

COST RATING

OVERALL RATING

RATE IT
Fill It In

TEQUILA
The Details

Brand Name **·····** Distiller

Age **·····** ABV/Proof **·····** Date

Distiller's Location **·····** Price per Glass/Bottle **·····** Tasting Location

NOSE
Choose All That Apply

SWEET
- ◯ brown sugar
- ◯ butterscotch
- ◯ caramel/toffee
- ◯ chocolate
- ◯ gingerbread
- ◯ honey
- ◯ maple syrup
- ◯ molasses

FRUITY
- ◯ apple

- ◯ berry
- ◯ cherry
- ◯ coconut
- ◯ dark fruit
- ◯ grapefruit
- ◯ lemon
- ◯ lime
- ◯ peach
- ◯ pineapple

WOODY & NUTTY
- ◯ almond

- ◯ char
- ◯ coffee
- ◯ oak
- ◯ roasted nuts
- ◯ smoke

VEGETAL & SPICY
- ◯ anise
- ◯ asparagus
- ◯ black pepper
- ◯ cinnamon
- ◯ clove

- ◯ dill
- ◯ gardenia
- ◯ geranium
- ◯ grass
- ◯ jasmine
- ◯ lavender
- ◯ menthol
- ◯ nutmeg
- ◯ pepper
- ◯ rose
- ◯ rosemary

- ◯ tea
- ◯ thyme
- ◯ tobacco

PUNGENT
- ◯ burnt match
- ◯ gasoline
- ◯ skunk
- ◯ wet wool
- ◯ whiskey

OTHER
·····

STYLE
Choose One

- ◯ Neat
- ◯ With Water
- ◯ Cocktail

COLOR
Circle One

TASTING WHEEL

Rate your tasting experience, 1 (lowest) to 5 (highest)

Categories (clockwise): Legs, Body, Balance, Sweet, Citrusy, Spicy, Earthy, Nutty, Woody, Smoky, Floral, Herbal, Pungency, Bite, Finish, Linger

Each axis rated 1, 2, 3, 4, 5

TASTING NOTES

Describe the First Sip

....

....

....

Describe the Third Sip

....

....

....

Describe the Body and Finish

....

....

....

What Is Most Striking About This Tequila?

....

....

....

Additional Notes

....

....

....

....

QUALITY RATING   **COST RATING**   **OVERALL RATING**

☆☆☆☆☆   

TEQUILA
The Details

Brand Name

Distiller

Age

ABV/Proof

Date

Distiller's Location

Price per Glass/Bottle

Tasting Location

NOSE
Choose All That Apply

SWEET
- ○ brown sugar
- ○ butterscotch
- ○ caramel/toffee
- ○ chocolate
- ○ gingerbread
- ○ honey
- ○ maple syrup
- ○ molasses

FRUITY
- ○ apple

- ○ berry
- ○ cherry
- ○ coconut
- ○ dark fruit
- ○ grapefruit
- ○ lemon
- ○ lime
- ○ peach
- ○ pineapple

WOODY & NUTTY
- ○ almond

- ○ char
- ○ coffee
- ○ oak
- ○ roasted nuts
- ○ smoke

VEGETAL & SPICY
- ○ anise
- ○ asparagus
- ○ black pepper
- ○ cinnamon
- ○ clove

- ○ dill
- ○ gardenia
- ○ geranium
- ○ grass
- ○ jasmine
- ○ lavender
- ○ menthol
- ○ nutmeg
- ○ pepper
- ○ rose
- ○ rosemary

- ○ tea
- ○ thyme
- ○ tobacco

PUNGENT
- ○ burnt match
- ○ gasoline
- ○ skunk
- ○ wet wool
- ○ whiskey

OTHER
....

STYLE
Choose One

- ○ Neat
- ○ With Water
- ○ Cocktail

COLOR
Circle One

TASTING WHEEL
Rate your tasting experience, 1 (lowest) to 5 (highest)

Legs, Body, Balance, Sweet, Citrusy, Spicy, Earthy, Nutty, Woody, Smoky, Floral, Herbal, Pungency, Bite, Finish, Linger

TASTING NOTES

Describe the First Sip

....

....

....

Describe the Third Sip

....

....

....

Describe the Body and Finish

....

....

....

What Is Most Striking About This Tequila?

....

....

....

Additional Notes

....

....

....

....

QUALITY RATING

COST RATING

OVERALL RATING

RATE IT

Fill It In

ENJOYING TEQUILA

TEQUILA
The Details

Brand Name

Distiller

Age

ABV/Proof

Date

Distiller's Location

Price per Glass/Bottle

Tasting Location

NOSE
Choose All That Apply

SWEET
- ○ brown sugar
- ○ butterscotch
- ○ caramel/toffee
- ○ chocolate
- ○ gingerbread
- ○ honey
- ○ maple syrup
- ○ molasses

FRUITY
- ○ apple

- ○ berry
- ○ cherry
- ○ coconut
- ○ dark fruit
- ○ grapefruit
- ○ lemon
- ○ lime
- ○ peach
- ○ pineapple

WOODY & NUTTY
- ○ almond

- ○ char
- ○ coffee
- ○ oak
- ○ roasted nuts
- ○ smoke

VEGETAL & SPICY
- ○ anise
- ○ asparagus
- ○ black pepper
- ○ cinnamon
- ○ clove

- ○ dill
- ○ gardenia
- ○ geranium
- ○ grass
- ○ jasmine
- ○ lavender
- ○ menthol
- ○ nutmeg
- ○ pepper
- ○ rose
- ○ rosemary

- ○ tea
- ○ thyme
- ○ tobacco

PUNGENT
- ○ burnt match
- ○ gasoline
- ○ skunk
- ○ wet wool
- ○ whiskey

OTHER

STYLE
Choose One

○ Neat

○ With Water

○ Cocktail

COLOR
Circle One

TASTING WHEEL

Rate your tasting experience, 1 (lowest) to 5 (highest)

Legs, Linger, Body, Finish, Balance, Bite, Sweet, Pungency, Citrusy, Herbal, Spicy, Floral, Earthy, Smoky, Woody, Nutty

98

TASTING NOTES

Describe the First Sip

....

....

....

Describe the Third Sip

....

....

....

Describe the Body and Finish

....

....

....

What Is Most Striking About This Tequila?

....

....

....

Additional Notes

....

....

....

....

GUIDED TASTING

Write It Out

QUALITY RATING	COST RATING	OVERALL RATING

RATE IT

Fill It In

TEQUILA
The Details

Brand Name

Distiller

Age

ABV/Proof

Date

Distiller's Location

Price per Glass/Bottle

Tasting Location

NOSE
Choose All That Apply

SWEET
- ○ brown sugar
- ○ butterscotch
- ○ caramel/toffee
- ○ chocolate
- ○ gingerbread
- ○ honey
- ○ maple syrup
- ○ molasses

FRUITY
- ○ apple

- ○ berry
- ○ cherry
- ○ coconut
- ○ dark fruit
- ○ grapefruit
- ○ lemon
- ○ lime
- ○ peach
- ○ pineapple

WOODY & NUTTY
- ○ almond

- ○ char
- ○ coffee
- ○ oak
- ○ roasted nuts
- ○ smoke

VEGETAL & SPICY
- ○ anise
- ○ asparagus
- ○ black pepper
- ○ cinnamon
- ○ clove

- ○ dill
- ○ gardenia
- ○ geranium
- ○ grass
- ○ jasmine
- ○ lavender
- ○ menthol
- ○ nutmeg
- ○ pepper
- ○ rose
- ○ rosemary

- ○ tea
- ○ thyme
- ○ tobacco

PUNGENT
- ○ burnt match
- ○ gasoline
- ○ skunk
- ○ wet wool
- ○ whiskey

OTHER

STYLE
Choose One

- ○ Neat
- ○ With Water
- ○ Cocktail

COLOR
Circle One

TASTING WHEEL

Rate your tasting experience, 1 (lowest) to 5 (highest)

TASTING NOTES

Describe the First Sip

....
....
....

Describe the Third Sip

....
....
....

Describe the Body and Finish

....
....
....

What Is Most Striking About This Tequila?

....
....
....

Additional Notes

....
....
....
....

GUIDED TASTING

Write It Out

QUALITY RATING

☆ ☆ ☆ ☆ ☆

COST RATING

OVERALL RATING

RATE IT

Fill It In

TEQUILA
The Details

Brand Name

Distiller

Age

ABV/Proof

Date

Distiller's Location

Price per Glass/Bottle

Tasting Location

NOSE
Choose All That Apply

SWEET
- O brown sugar
- O butterscotch
- O caramel/toffee
- O chocolate
- O gingerbread
- O honey
- O maple syrup
- O molasses

FRUITY
- O apple

- O berry
- O cherry
- O coconut
- O dark fruit
- O grapefruit
- O lemon
- O lime
- O peach
- O pineapple

WOODY & NUTTY
- O almond

- O char
- O coffee
- O oak
- O roasted nuts
- O smoke

VEGETAL & SPICY
- O anise
- O asparagus
- O black pepper
- O cinnamon
- O clove

- O dill
- O gardenia
- O geranium
- O grass
- O jasmine
- O lavender
- O menthol
- O nutmeg
- O pepper
- O rose
- O rosemary

- O tea
- O thyme
- O tobacco

PUNGENT
- O burnt match
- O gasoline
- O skunk
- O wet wool
- O whiskey

OTHER

STYLE
Choose One

- O Neat
- O With Water
- O Cocktail

COLOR
Circle One

TASTING WHEEL

Rate your tasting experience, 1 (lowest) to 5 (highest)

Legs
Linger
Body
Finish
Balance
Bite
Sweet
Pungency
Citrusy
Herbal
Spicy
Floral
Earthy
Smoky
Woody
Nutty

TASTING NOTES

Describe the First Sip

....

....

....

Describe the Third Sip

....

....

....

Describe the Body and Finish

....

....

....

What Is Most Striking About This Tequila?

....

....

....

Additional Notes

....

....

....

....

GUIDED TASTING
Write It Out

QUALITY RATING
☆ ☆ ☆ ☆ ☆

COST RATING
Ⓢ Ⓢ Ⓢ Ⓢ Ⓢ

OVERALL RATING

RATE IT
Fill It In

ENJOYING TEQUILA

TEQUILA — The Details

Brand Name

Distiller

Age

ABV/Proof

Date

Distiller's Location

Price per Glass/Bottle

Tasting Location

NOSE
Choose All That Apply

SWEET
- ○ brown sugar
- ○ butterscotch
- ○ caramel/toffee
- ○ chocolate
- ○ gingerbread
- ○ honey
- ○ maple syrup
- ○ molasses

FRUITY
- ○ apple
- ○ berry
- ○ cherry
- ○ coconut
- ○ dark fruit
- ○ grapefruit
- ○ lemon
- ○ lime
- ○ peach
- ○ pineapple

WOODY & NUTTY
- ○ almond
- ○ char
- ○ coffee
- ○ oak
- ○ roasted nuts
- ○ smoke

VEGETAL & SPICY
- ○ anise
- ○ asparagus
- ○ black pepper
- ○ cinnamon
- ○ clove
- ○ dill
- ○ gardenia
- ○ geranium
- ○ grass
- ○ jasmine
- ○ lavender
- ○ menthol
- ○ nutmeg
- ○ pepper
- ○ rose
- ○ rosemary
- ○ tea
- ○ thyme
- ○ tobacco

PUNGENT
- ○ burnt match
- ○ gasoline
- ○ skunk
- ○ wet wool
- ○ whiskey

OTHER
....

STYLE
Choose One
- ○ Neat
- ○ With Water
- ○ Cocktail

TASTING WHEEL
Rate your tasting experience, 1 (lowest) to 5 (highest)

Legs, Body, Balance, Sweet, Citrusy, Spicy, Earthy, Nutty, Woody, Smoky, Floral, Herbal, Pungency, Bite, Finish, Linger

COLOR
Circle One

TASTING NOTES

Describe the First Sip

....

....

....

Describe the Third Sip

....

....

....

Describe the Body and Finish

....

....

....

What Is Most Striking About This Tequila?

....

....

....

Additional Notes

....

....

....

....

GUIDED TASTING

Write It Out

QUALITY RATING

☆ ☆ ☆ ☆ ☆

COST RATING

OVERALL RATING

RATE IT

Fill It In

TEQUILA
The Details

Brand Name .... Distiller

Age .... ABV/Proof .... Date

Distiller's Location .... Price per Glass/Bottle .... Tasting Location

NOSE
Choose All That Apply

SWEET
- ○ brown sugar
- ○ butterscotch
- ○ caramel/toffee
- ○ chocolate
- ○ gingerbread
- ○ honey
- ○ maple syrup
- ○ molasses

FRUITY
- ○ apple

- ○ berry
- ○ cherry
- ○ coconut
- ○ dark fruit
- ○ grapefruit
- ○ lemon
- ○ lime
- ○ peach
- ○ pineapple

WOODY & NUTTY
- ○ almond

- ○ char
- ○ coffee
- ○ oak
- ○ roasted nuts
- ○ smoke

VEGETAL & SPICY
- ○ anise
- ○ asparagus
- ○ black pepper
- ○ cinnamon
- ○ clove

- ○ dill
- ○ gardenia
- ○ geranium
- ○ grass
- ○ jasmine
- ○ lavender
- ○ menthol
- ○ nutmeg
- ○ pepper
- ○ rose
- ○ rosemary

- ○ tea
- ○ thyme
- ○ tobacco

PUNGENT
- ○ burnt match
- ○ gasoline
- ○ skunk
- ○ wet wool
- ○ whiskey

OTHER
....

STYLE
Choose One

- ○ Neat
- ○ With Water
- ○ Cocktail

COLOR
Circle One

TASTING WHEEL
Rate your tasting experience, 1 (lowest) to 5 (highest)

TASTING NOTES

Describe the First Sip

....
....
....

Describe the Third Sip

....
....
....

Describe the Body and Finish

....
....
....

What Is Most Striking About This Tequila?

....
....
....

Additional Notes

....
....
....
....

QUALITY RATING   **COST RATING**   **OVERALL RATING**

ENJOYING TEQUILA

TEQUILA
The Details

Brand Name   Distiller

Age   ABV/Proof   Date

Distiller's Location   Price per Glass/Bottle   Tasting Location

NOSE
Choose All That Apply

SWEET
- ○ brown sugar
- ○ butterscotch
- ○ caramel/toffee
- ○ chocolate
- ○ gingerbread
- ○ honey
- ○ maple syrup
- ○ molasses

FRUITY
- ○ apple

- ○ berry
- ○ cherry
- ○ coconut
- ○ dark fruit
- ○ grapefruit
- ○ lemon
- ○ lime
- ○ peach
- ○ pineapple

WOODY & NUTTY
- ○ almond

- ○ char
- ○ coffee
- ○ oak
- ○ roasted nuts
- ○ smoke

VEGETAL & SPICY
- ○ anise
- ○ asparagus
- ○ black pepper
- ○ cinnamon
- ○ clove

- ○ dill
- ○ gardenia
- ○ geranium
- ○ grass
- ○ jasmine
- ○ lavender
- ○ menthol
- ○ nutmeg
- ○ pepper
- ○ rose
- ○ rosemary

- ○ tea
- ○ thyme
- ○ tobacco

PUNGENT
- ○ burnt match
- ○ gasoline
- ○ skunk
- ○ wet wool
- ○ whiskey

OTHER

STYLE
Choose One

- ○ Neat
- ○ With Water
- ○ Cocktail

TASTING WHEEL

Rate your tasting experience, 1 (lowest) to 5 (highest)

COLOR
Circle One

TASTING NOTES

Describe the First Sip

....

....

....

Describe the Third Sip

....

....

....

Describe the Body and Finish

....

....

....

What Is Most Striking About This Tequila?

....

....

....

Additional Notes

....

....

....

....

QUALITY RATING

☆ ☆ ☆ ☆ ☆

COST RATING

OVERALL RATING

TEQUILA
The Details

Brand Name

Distiller

Age

ABV/Proof

Date

Distiller's Location

Price per Glass/Bottle

Tasting Location

NOSE
Choose All That Apply

SWEET
- ○ brown sugar
- ○ butterscotch
- ○ caramel/toffee
- ○ chocolate
- ○ gingerbread
- ○ honey
- ○ maple syrup
- ○ molasses

FRUITY
- ○ apple

- ○ berry
- ○ cherry
- ○ coconut
- ○ dark fruit
- ○ grapefruit
- ○ lemon
- ○ lime
- ○ peach
- ○ pineapple

WOODY & NUTTY
- ○ almond

- ○ char
- ○ coffee
- ○ oak
- ○ roasted nuts
- ○ smoke

VEGETAL & SPICY
- ○ anise
- ○ asparagus
- ○ black pepper
- ○ cinnamon
- ○ clove

- ○ dill
- ○ gardenia
- ○ geranium
- ○ grass
- ○ jasmine
- ○ lavender
- ○ menthol
- ○ nutmeg
- ○ pepper
- ○ rose
- ○ rosemary

- ○ tea
- ○ thyme
- ○ tobacco

PUNGENT
- ○ burnt match
- ○ gasoline
- ○ skunk
- ○ wet wool
- ○ whiskey

OTHER

STYLE
Choose One

- ○ Neat
- ○ With Water
- ○ Cocktail

COLOR
Circle One

TASTING WHEEL

Rate your tasting experience, 1 (lowest) to 5 (highest)

TASTING NOTES

Describe the First Sip

....

....

....

Describe the Third Sip

....

....

....

Describe the Body and Finish

....

....

....

What Is Most Striking About This Tequila?

....

....

....

Additional Notes

....

....

....

....

QUALITY RATING

☆ ☆ ☆ ☆ ☆

COST RATING

OVERALL RATING

TEQUILA
The Details

Brand Name

Distiller

Age

ABV/Proof

Date

Distiller's Location

Price per Glass/Bottle

Tasting Location

NOSE
Choose All That Apply

SWEET
- ○ brown sugar
- ○ butterscotch
- ○ caramel/toffee
- ○ chocolate
- ○ gingerbread
- ○ honey
- ○ maple syrup
- ○ molasses

FRUITY
- ○ apple

- ○ berry
- ○ cherry
- ○ coconut
- ○ dark fruit
- ○ grapefruit
- ○ lemon
- ○ lime
- ○ peach
- ○ pineapple

WOODY & NUTTY
- ○ almond

- ○ char
- ○ coffee
- ○ oak
- ○ roasted nuts
- ○ smoke

VEGETAL & SPICY
- ○ anise
- ○ asparagus
- ○ black pepper
- ○ cinnamon
- ○ clove

- ○ dill
- ○ gardenia
- ○ geranium
- ○ grass
- ○ jasmine
- ○ lavender
- ○ menthol
- ○ nutmeg
- ○ pepper
- ○ rose
- ○ rosemary

- ○ tea
- ○ thyme
- ○ tobacco

PUNGENT
- ○ burnt match
- ○ gasoline
- ○ skunk
- ○ wet wool
- ○ whiskey

OTHER

STYLE
Choose One

- ○ Neat
- ○ With Water
- ○ Cocktail

COLOR
Circle One

TASTING WHEEL
Rate your tasting experience, 1 (lowest) to 5 (highest)

TASTING NOTES

Describe the First Sip

....

....

....

Describe the Third Sip

....

....

....

Describe the Body and Finish

....

....

....

What Is Most Striking About This Tequila?

....

....

....

Additional Notes

....

....

....

....

QUALITY RATING

COST RATING

OVERALL RATING

TEQUILA
The Details

Brand Name

Distiller

Age

ABV/Proof

Date

Distiller's Location

Price per Glass/Bottle

Tasting Location

NOSE
Choose All That Apply

SWEET
- ○ brown sugar
- ○ butterscotch
- ○ caramel/toffee
- ○ chocolate
- ○ gingerbread
- ○ honey
- ○ maple syrup
- ○ molasses

FRUITY
- ○ apple

- ○ berry
- ○ cherry
- ○ coconut
- ○ dark fruit
- ○ grapefruit
- ○ lemon
- ○ lime
- ○ peach
- ○ pineapple

WOODY & NUTTY
- ○ almond

- ○ char
- ○ coffee
- ○ oak
- ○ roasted nuts
- ○ smoke

VEGETAL & SPICY
- ○ anise
- ○ asparagus
- ○ black pepper
- ○ cinnamon
- ○ clove

- ○ dill
- ○ gardenia
- ○ geranium
- ○ grass
- ○ jasmine
- ○ lavender
- ○ menthol
- ○ nutmeg
- ○ pepper
- ○ rose
- ○ rosemary

- ○ tea
- ○ thyme
- ○ tobacco

PUNGENT
- ○ burnt match
- ○ gasoline
- ○ skunk
- ○ wet wool
- ○ whiskey

OTHER
....

STYLE
Choose One

- ○ Neat
- ○ With Water
- ○ Cocktail

COLOR
Circle One

TASTING WHEEL

Rate your tasting experience, 1 (lowest) to 5 (highest)

Legs · Body · Balance · Sweet · Citrusy · Spicy · Earthy · Nutty · Woody · Smoky · Floral · Herbal · Pungency · Bite · Finish · Linger

TASTING NOTES

Describe the First Sip

....

....

....

Describe the Third Sip

....

....

....

Describe the Body and Finish

....

....

....

What Is Most Striking About This Tequila?

....

....

....

Additional Notes

....

....

....

....

GUIDED TASTING

Write It Out

QUALITY RATING	COST RATING	OVERALL RATING
☆ ☆ ☆ ☆ ☆		

RATE IT

Fill It In

TEQUILA
The Details

Brand Name

Distiller

Age

ABV/Proof

Date

Distiller's Location

Price per Glass/Bottle

Tasting Location

NOSE
Choose All That Apply

SWEET
- ○ brown sugar
- ○ butterscotch
- ○ caramel/toffee
- ○ chocolate
- ○ gingerbread
- ○ honey
- ○ maple syrup
- ○ molasses

FRUITY
- ○ apple

- ○ berry
- ○ cherry
- ○ coconut
- ○ dark fruit
- ○ grapefruit
- ○ lemon
- ○ lime
- ○ peach
- ○ pineapple

WOODY & NUTTY
- ○ almond

- ○ char
- ○ coffee
- ○ oak
- ○ roasted nuts
- ○ smoke

VEGETAL & SPICY
- ○ anise
- ○ asparagus
- ○ black pepper
- ○ cinnamon
- ○ clove

- ○ dill
- ○ gardenia
- ○ geranium
- ○ grass
- ○ jasmine
- ○ lavender
- ○ menthol
- ○ nutmeg
- ○ pepper
- ○ rose
- ○ rosemary

- ○ tea
- ○ thyme
- ○ tobacco

PUNGENT
- ○ burnt match
- ○ gasoline
- ○ skunk
- ○ wet wool
- ○ whiskey

OTHER

STYLE
Choose One

- ○ Neat
- ○ With Water
- ○ Cocktail

COLOR
Circle One

TASTING WHEEL

Rate your tasting experience, 1 (lowest) to 5 (highest)

TASTING NOTES

Describe the First Sip

....

....

....

Describe the Third Sip

....

....

....

Describe the Body and Finish

....

....

....

What Is Most Striking About This Tequila?

....

....

....

Additional Notes

....

....

....

....

GUIDED TASTING

Write It Out

QUALITY RATING	COST RATING	OVERALL RATING	
☆ ☆ ☆ ☆ ☆			RATE IT / Fill It In

TEQUILA
The Details

Brand Name   **Distiller**

Age   **ABV/Proof**   **Date**

Distiller's Location   **Price per Glass/Bottle**   **Tasting Location**

NOSE
Choose All That Apply

SWEET
- ○ brown sugar
- ○ butterscotch
- ○ caramel/toffee
- ○ chocolate
- ○ gingerbread
- ○ honey
- ○ maple syrup
- ○ molasses

FRUITY
- ○ apple

- ○ berry
- ○ cherry
- ○ coconut
- ○ dark fruit
- ○ grapefruit
- ○ lemon
- ○ lime
- ○ peach
- ○ pineapple

WOODY & NUTTY
- ○ almond

- ○ char
- ○ coffee
- ○ oak
- ○ roasted nuts
- ○ smoke

VEGETAL & SPICY
- ○ anise
- ○ asparagus
- ○ black pepper
- ○ cinnamon
- ○ clove

- ○ dill
- ○ gardenia
- ○ geranium
- ○ grass
- ○ jasmine
- ○ lavender
- ○ menthol
- ○ nutmeg
- ○ pepper
- ○ rose
- ○ rosemary

- ○ tea
- ○ thyme
- ○ tobacco

PUNGENT
- ○ burnt match
- ○ gasoline
- ○ skunk
- ○ wet wool
- ○ whiskey

OTHER
....

STYLE
Choose One

- ○ Neat
- ○ With Water
- ○ Cocktail

COLOR
Circle One

TASTING WHEEL

Rate your tasting experience, 1 (lowest) to 5 (highest)

TASTING NOTES

Describe the First Sip

....
....
....

Describe the Third Sip

....
....
....

Describe the Body and Finish

....
....
....

What Is Most Striking About This Tequila?

....
....
....

Additional Notes

....
....
....
....

GUIDED TASTING

Write It Out

QUALITY RATING

☆ ☆ ☆ ☆ ☆

COST RATING

OVERALL RATING

RATE IT

Fill It In

ENJOYING TEQUILA

TEQUILA
The Details

Brand Name

Distiller

Age

ABV/Proof

Date

Distiller's Location

Price per Glass/Bottle

Tasting Location

NOSE
Choose All That Apply

SWEET
- ◯ brown sugar
- ◯ butterscotch
- ◯ caramel/toffee
- ◯ chocolate
- ◯ gingerbread
- ◯ honey
- ◯ maple syrup
- ◯ molasses

FRUITY
- ◯ apple

- ◯ berry
- ◯ cherry
- ◯ coconut
- ◯ dark fruit
- ◯ grapefruit
- ◯ lemon
- ◯ lime
- ◯ peach
- ◯ pineapple

WOODY & NUTTY
- ◯ almond

- ◯ char
- ◯ coffee
- ◯ oak
- ◯ roasted nuts
- ◯ smoke

VEGETAL & SPICY
- ◯ anise
- ◯ asparagus
- ◯ black pepper
- ◯ cinnamon
- ◯ clove

- ◯ dill
- ◯ gardenia
- ◯ geranium
- ◯ grass
- ◯ jasmine
- ◯ lavender
- ◯ menthol
- ◯ nutmeg
- ◯ pepper
- ◯ rose
- ◯ rosemary

- ◯ tea
- ◯ thyme
- ◯ tobacco

PUNGENT
- ◯ burnt match
- ◯ gasoline
- ◯ skunk
- ◯ wet wool
- ◯ whiskey

OTHER

STYLE
Choose One

- ◯ Neat
- ◯ With Water
- ◯ Cocktail

COLOR
Circle One

TASTING WHEEL

Rate your tasting experience, 1 (lowest) to 5 (highest)

Legs · Body · Balance · Sweet · Citrusy · Spicy · Earthy · Nutty · Woody · Smoky · Floral · Herbal · Pungency · Bite · Finish · Linger

TASTING NOTES

Describe the First Sip

....

....

....

Describe the Third Sip

....

....

....

Describe the Body and Finish

....

....

....

What Is Most Striking About This Tequila?

....

....

....

Additional Notes

....

....

....

....

GUIDED TASTING
Write It Out

QUALITY RATING   COST RATING   OVERALL RATING

RATE IT
Fill It In

ENJOYING TEQUILA

TEQUILA — The Details

Brand Name	Distiller	
Age	ABV/Proof	Date
Distiller's Location	Price per Glass/Bottle	Tasting Location

NOSE — Choose All That Apply

SWEET
- O brown sugar
- O butterscotch
- O caramel/toffee
- O chocolate
- O gingerbread
- O honey
- O maple syrup
- O molasses

FRUITY
- O apple
- O berry
- O cherry
- O coconut
- O dark fruit
- O grapefruit
- O lemon
- O lime
- O peach
- O pineapple

WOODY & NUTTY
- O almond
- O char
- O coffee
- O oak
- O roasted nuts
- O smoke

VEGETAL & SPICY
- O anise
- O asparagus
- O black pepper
- O cinnamon
- O clove
- O dill
- O gardenia
- O geranium
- O grass
- O jasmine
- O lavender
- O menthol
- O nutmeg
- O pepper
- O rose
- O rosemary
- O tea
- O thyme
- O tobacco

PUNGENT
- O burnt match
- O gasoline
- O skunk
- O wet wool
- O whiskey

OTHER
....

STYLE — Choose One

- O Neat
- O With Water
- O Cocktail

TASTING WHEEL

Rate your tasting experience, 1 (lowest) to 5 (highest)

Spokes: Legs, Body, Balance, Sweet, Citrusy, Spicy, Earthy, Nutty, Woody, Smoky, Floral, Herbal, Pungency, Bite, Finish, Linger

COLOR — Circle One

TASTING NOTES

Describe the First Sip

....

....

....

Describe the Third Sip

....

....

....

Describe the Body and Finish

....

....

....

What Is Most Striking About This Tequila?

....

....

....

Additional Notes

....

....

....

....

GUIDED TASTING

Write It Out

QUALITY RATING	COST RATING	OVERALL RATING
☆☆☆☆☆		

RATE IT

Fill It In

TEQUILA
The Details

Brand Name .... Distiller

Age .... ABV/Proof .... Date

Distiller's Location .... Price per Glass/Bottle .... Tasting Location

NOSE
Choose All That Apply

SWEET
- ◯ brown sugar
- ◯ butterscotch
- ◯ caramel/toffee
- ◯ chocolate
- ◯ gingerbread
- ◯ honey
- ◯ maple syrup
- ◯ molasses

FRUITY
- ◯ apple

- ◯ berry
- ◯ cherry
- ◯ coconut
- ◯ dark fruit
- ◯ grapefruit
- ◯ lemon
- ◯ lime
- ◯ peach
- ◯ pineapple

WOODY & NUTTY
- ◯ almond

- ◯ char
- ◯ coffee
- ◯ oak
- ◯ roasted nuts
- ◯ smoke

VEGETAL & SPICY
- ◯ anise
- ◯ asparagus
- ◯ black pepper
- ◯ cinnamon
- ◯ clove

- ◯ dill
- ◯ gardenia
- ◯ geranium
- ◯ grass
- ◯ jasmine
- ◯ lavender
- ◯ menthol
- ◯ nutmeg
- ◯ pepper
- ◯ rose
- ◯ rosemary

- ◯ tea
- ◯ thyme
- ◯ tobacco

PUNGENT
- ◯ burnt match
- ◯ gasoline
- ◯ skunk
- ◯ wet wool
- ◯ whiskey

OTHER
....

STYLE
Choose One

- ◯ Neat
- ◯ With Water
- ◯ Cocktail

COLOR
Circle One

TASTING WHEEL

Rate your tasting experience, 1 (lowest) to 5 (highest)

Legs, Body, Balance, Sweet, Citrusy, Spicy, Earthy, Nutty, Woody, Smoky, Floral, Herbal, Pungency, Bite, Finish, Linger

TASTING NOTES

Describe the First Sip

....

....

....

Describe the Third Sip

....

....

....

Describe the Body and Finish

....

....

....

What Is Most Striking About This Tequila?

....

....

....

Additional Notes

....

....

....

....

QUALITY RATING

☆ ☆ ☆ ☆ ☆

COST RATING

OVERALL RATING

TEQUILA
The Details

Brand Name

Distiller

Age

ABV/Proof

Date

Distiller's Location

Price per Glass/Bottle

Tasting Location

NOSE
Choose All That Apply

SWEET
- ○ brown sugar
- ○ butterscotch
- ○ caramel/toffee
- ○ chocolate
- ○ gingerbread
- ○ honey
- ○ maple syrup
- ○ molasses

FRUITY
- ○ apple

- ○ berry
- ○ cherry
- ○ coconut
- ○ dark fruit
- ○ grapefruit
- ○ lemon
- ○ lime
- ○ peach
- ○ pineapple

WOODY & NUTTY
- ○ almond

- ○ char
- ○ coffee
- ○ oak
- ○ roasted nuts
- ○ smoke

VEGETAL & SPICY
- ○ anise
- ○ asparagus
- ○ black pepper
- ○ cinnamon
- ○ clove

- ○ dill
- ○ gardenia
- ○ geranium
- ○ grass
- ○ jasmine
- ○ lavender
- ○ menthol
- ○ nutmeg
- ○ pepper
- ○ rose
- ○ rosemary

- ○ tea
- ○ thyme
- ○ tobacco

PUNGENT
- ○ burnt match
- ○ gasoline
- ○ skunk
- ○ wet wool
- ○ whiskey

OTHER
....

STYLE
Choose One

- ○ Neat
- ○ With Water
- ○ Cocktail

COLOR
Circle One

TASTING WHEEL

Rate your tasting experience, 1 (lowest) to 5 (highest)

TASTING NOTES

Describe the First Sip

....

....

....

Describe the Third Sip

....

....

....

Describe the Body and Finish

....

....

....

What Is Most Striking About This Tequila?

....

....

....

Additional Notes

....

....

....

....

GUIDED TASTING

Write It Out

QUALITY RATING

☆ ☆ ☆ ☆ ☆

COST RATING

ⓢ ⓢ ⓢ ⓢ ⓢ

OVERALL RATING

RATE IT

Fill It In

TEQUILA
The Details

Brand Name

Distiller

Age

ABV/Proof

Date

Distiller's Location

Price per Glass/Bottle

Tasting Location

NOSE
Choose All That Apply

SWEET
- ○ brown sugar
- ○ butterscotch
- ○ caramel/toffee
- ○ chocolate
- ○ gingerbread
- ○ honey
- ○ maple syrup
- ○ molasses

FRUITY
- ○ apple

- ○ berry
- ○ cherry
- ○ coconut
- ○ dark fruit
- ○ grapefruit
- ○ lemon
- ○ lime
- ○ peach
- ○ pineapple

WOODY & NUTTY
- ○ almond

- ○ char
- ○ coffee
- ○ oak
- ○ roasted nuts
- ○ smoke

VEGETAL & SPICY
- ○ anise
- ○ asparagus
- ○ black pepper
- ○ cinnamon
- ○ clove

- ○ dill
- ○ gardenia
- ○ geranium
- ○ grass
- ○ jasmine
- ○ lavender
- ○ menthol
- ○ nutmeg
- ○ pepper
- ○ rose
- ○ rosemary

- ○ tea
- ○ thyme
- ○ tobacco

PUNGENT
- ○ burnt match
- ○ gasoline
- ○ skunk
- ○ wet wool
- ○ whiskey

OTHER
....

STYLE
Choose One

- ○ Neat
- ○ With Water
- ○ Cocktail

COLOR
Circle One

TASTING WHEEL
Rate your tasting experience, 1 (lowest) to 5 (highest)

Legs · Body · Balance · Sweet · Citrusy · Spicy · Earthy · Nutty · Woody · Smoky · Floral · Herbal · Pungency · Bite · Finish · Linger

TASTING NOTES

Describe the First Sip

....

....

....

Describe the Third Sip

....

....

....

Describe the Body and Finish

....

....

....

What Is Most Striking About This Tequila?

....

....

....

Additional Notes

....

....

....

....

RATE IT

Fill It In

QUALITY RATING

☆ ☆ ☆ ☆ ☆

COST RATING

OVERALL RATING

TEQUILA
The Details

Brand Name .... Distiller ....

Age .... ABV/Proof .... Date ....

Distiller's Location .... Price per Glass/Bottle .... Tasting Location ....

NOSE
Choose All That Apply

SWEET
- ○ brown sugar
- ○ butterscotch
- ○ caramel/toffee
- ○ chocolate
- ○ gingerbread
- ○ honey
- ○ maple syrup
- ○ molasses

FRUITY
- ○ apple

- ○ berry
- ○ cherry
- ○ coconut
- ○ dark fruit
- ○ grapefruit
- ○ lemon
- ○ lime
- ○ peach
- ○ pineapple

WOODY & NUTTY
- ○ almond

- ○ char
- ○ coffee
- ○ oak
- ○ roasted nuts
- ○ smoke

VEGETAL & SPICY
- ○ anise
- ○ asparagus
- ○ black pepper
- ○ cinnamon
- ○ clove

- ○ dill
- ○ gardenia
- ○ geranium
- ○ grass
- ○ jasmine
- ○ lavender
- ○ menthol
- ○ nutmeg
- ○ pepper
- ○ rose
- ○ rosemary

- ○ tea
- ○ thyme
- ○ tobacco

PUNGENT
- ○ burnt match
- ○ gasoline
- ○ skunk
- ○ wet wool
- ○ whiskey

OTHER
....

STYLE
Choose One

- ○ Neat
- ○ With Water
- ○ Cocktail

COLOR
Circle One

TASTING WHEEL
Rate your tasting experience, 1 (lowest) to 5 (highest)

TASTING NOTES

Describe the First Sip

....

....

....

Describe the Third Sip

....

....

....

Describe the Body and Finish

....

....

....

What Is Most Striking About This Tequila?

....

....

....

Additional Notes

....

....

....

....

GUIDED TASTING

Write It Out

QUALITY RATING

☆ ☆ ☆ ☆ ☆

COST RATING

OVERALL RATING

RATE IT

Fill It In

ENJOYING TEQUILA

TEQUILA — The Details

Brand Name   **Distiller**

Age   **ABV/Proof**   **Date**

Distiller's Location   **Price per Glass/Bottle**   **Tasting Location**

NOSE
Choose All That Apply

SWEET
- brown sugar
- butterscotch
- caramel/toffee
- chocolate
- gingerbread
- honey
- maple syrup
- molasses

FRUITY
- apple

- berry
- cherry
- coconut
- dark fruit
- grapefruit
- lemon
- lime
- peach
- pineapple

WOODY & NUTTY
- almond

- char
- coffee
- oak
- roasted nuts
- smoke

VEGETAL & SPICY
- anise
- asparagus
- black pepper
- cinnamon
- clove

- dill
- gardenia
- geranium
- grass
- jasmine
- lavender
- menthol
- nutmeg
- pepper
- rose
- rosemary

- tea
- thyme
- tobacco

PUNGENT
- burnt match
- gasoline
- skunk
- wet wool
- whiskey

OTHER
....

STYLE
Choose One
- Neat
- With Water
- Cocktail

TASTING WHEEL
Rate your tasting experience, 1 (lowest) to 5 (highest)

Legs, Body, Balance, Sweet, Citrusy, Spicy, Earthy, Nutty, Woody, Smoky, Floral, Herbal, Pungency, Bite, Finish, Linger

COLOR
Circle One

TASTING NOTES

Describe the First Sip

....

....

....

Describe the Third Sip

....

....

....

Describe the Body and Finish

....

....

....

What Is Most Striking About This Tequila?

....

....

....

Additional Notes

....

....

....

....

GUIDED TASTING
Write It Out

QUALITY RATING	COST RATING	OVERALL RATING
☆☆☆☆☆		

RATE IT
Fill It In

TEQUILA
The Details

Brand Name

Distiller

Age

ABV/Proof

Date

Distiller's Location

Price per Glass/Bottle

Tasting Location

NOSE
Choose All That Apply

SWEET
- ○ brown sugar
- ○ butterscotch
- ○ caramel/toffee
- ○ chocolate
- ○ gingerbread
- ○ honey
- ○ maple syrup
- ○ molasses

FRUITY
- ○ apple

- ○ berry
- ○ cherry
- ○ coconut
- ○ dark fruit
- ○ grapefruit
- ○ lemon
- ○ lime
- ○ peach
- ○ pineapple

WOODY & NUTTY
- ○ almond

- ○ char
- ○ coffee
- ○ oak
- ○ roasted nuts
- ○ smoke

VEGETAL & SPICY
- ○ anise
- ○ asparagus
- ○ black pepper
- ○ cinnamon
- ○ clove

- ○ dill
- ○ gardenia
- ○ geranium
- ○ grass
- ○ jasmine
- ○ lavender
- ○ menthol
- ○ nutmeg
- ○ pepper
- ○ rose
- ○ rosemary

- ○ tea
- ○ thyme
- ○ tobacco

PUNGENT
- ○ burnt match
- ○ gasoline
- ○ skunk
- ○ wet wool
- ○ whiskey

OTHER

STYLE
Choose One

- ○ Neat
- ○ With Water
- ○ Cocktail

COLOR
Circle One

TASTING WHEEL

Rate your tasting experience, 1 (lowest) to 5 (highest)

Legs, Body, Balance, Sweet, Citrusy, Spicy, Earthy, Nutty, Woody, Smoky, Floral, Herbal, Pungency, Bite, Finish, Linger

TASTING NOTES

Describe the First Sip

....

....

....

Describe the Third Sip

....

....

....

Describe the Body and Finish

....

....

....

What Is Most Striking About This Tequila?

....

....

....

Additional Notes

....

....

....

....

QUALITY RATING	COST RATING	OVERALL RATING
☆☆☆☆☆		

TEQUILA

The Details

Brand Name

Distiller

Age

ABV/Proof

Date

Distiller's Location

Price per Glass/Bottle

Tasting Location

NOSE

Choose All That Apply

SWEET
- ○ brown sugar
- ○ butterscotch
- ○ caramel/toffee
- ○ chocolate
- ○ gingerbread
- ○ honey
- ○ maple syrup
- ○ molasses

FRUITY
- ○ apple

- ○ berry
- ○ cherry
- ○ coconut
- ○ dark fruit
- ○ grapefruit
- ○ lemon
- ○ lime
- ○ peach
- ○ pineapple

WOODY & NUTTY
- ○ almond

- ○ char
- ○ coffee
- ○ oak
- ○ roasted nuts
- ○ smoke

VEGETAL & SPICY
- ○ anise
- ○ asparagus
- ○ black pepper
- ○ cinnamon
- ○ clove

- ○ dill
- ○ gardenia
- ○ geranium
- ○ grass
- ○ jasmine
- ○ lavender
- ○ menthol
- ○ nutmeg
- ○ pepper
- ○ rose
- ○ rosemary

- ○ tea
- ○ thyme
- ○ tobacco

PUNGENT
- ○ burnt match
- ○ gasoline
- ○ skunk
- ○ wet wool
- ○ whiskey

OTHER

STYLE

Choose One

- ○ Neat
- ○ With Water
- ○ Cocktail

COLOR

Circle One

TASTING WHEEL

Rate your tasting experience, 1 (lowest) to 5 (highest)

TASTING NOTES

Describe the First Sip

....

....

....

Describe the Third Sip

....

....

....

Describe the Body and Finish

....

....

....

What Is Most Striking About This Tequila?

....

....

....

Additional Notes

....

....

....

....

QUALITY RATING   COST RATING   OVERALL RATING

☆☆☆☆☆   ⓢ ⓢ ⓢ ⓢ ⓢ

ENJOYING TEQUILA

TEQUILA
The Details

Brand Name .... **Distiller** ....

Age .... **ABV/Proof** .... **Date** ....

Distiller's Location .... **Price per Glass/Bottle** .... **Tasting Location** ....

NOSE
Choose All That Apply

SWEET
- ○ brown sugar
- ○ butterscotch
- ○ caramel/toffee
- ○ chocolate
- ○ gingerbread
- ○ honey
- ○ maple syrup
- ○ molasses

FRUITY
- ○ apple

- ○ berry
- ○ cherry
- ○ coconut
- ○ dark fruit
- ○ grapefruit
- ○ lemon
- ○ lime
- ○ peach
- ○ pineapple

WOODY & NUTTY
- ○ almond

- ○ char
- ○ coffee
- ○ oak
- ○ roasted nuts
- ○ smoke

VEGETAL & SPICY
- ○ anise
- ○ asparagus
- ○ black pepper
- ○ cinnamon
- ○ clove

- ○ dill
- ○ gardenia
- ○ geranium
- ○ grass
- ○ jasmine
- ○ lavender
- ○ menthol
- ○ nutmeg
- ○ pepper
- ○ rose
- ○ rosemary

- ○ tea
- ○ thyme
- ○ tobacco

PUNGENT
- ○ burnt match
- ○ gasoline
- ○ skunk
- ○ wet wool
- ○ whiskey

OTHER
....

STYLE
Choose One

- ○ Neat
- ○ With Water
- ○ Cocktail

COLOR
Circle One

TASTING WHEEL

Rate your tasting experience, 1 (lowest) to 5 (highest)

Legs, Body, Balance, Sweet, Citrusy, Spicy, Earthy, Nutty, Woody, Smoky, Floral, Herbal, Pungency, Bite, Finish, Linger

TASTING NOTES

Describe the First Sip

....

....

....

Describe the Third Sip

....

....

....

Describe the Body and Finish

....

....

....

What Is Most Striking About This Tequila?

....

....

....

Additional Notes

....

....

....

....

QUALITY RATING

COST RATING

OVERALL RATING

ENJOYING TEQUILA

TEQUILA
The Details

Brand Name

Distiller

Age

ABV/Proof

Date

Distiller's Location

Price per Glass/Bottle

Tasting Location

NOSE
Choose All That Apply

SWEET
- ◯ brown sugar
- ◯ butterscotch
- ◯ caramel/toffee
- ◯ chocolate
- ◯ gingerbread
- ◯ honey
- ◯ maple syrup
- ◯ molasses

FRUITY
- ◯ apple

- ◯ berry
- ◯ cherry
- ◯ coconut
- ◯ dark fruit
- ◯ grapefruit
- ◯ lemon
- ◯ lime
- ◯ peach
- ◯ pineapple

WOODY & NUTTY
- ◯ almond

- ◯ char
- ◯ coffee
- ◯ oak
- ◯ roasted nuts
- ◯ smoke

VEGETAL & SPICY
- ◯ anise
- ◯ asparagus
- ◯ black pepper
- ◯ cinnamon
- ◯ clove

- ◯ dill
- ◯ gardenia
- ◯ geranium
- ◯ grass
- ◯ jasmine
- ◯ lavender
- ◯ menthol
- ◯ nutmeg
- ◯ pepper
- ◯ rose
- ◯ rosemary

- ◯ tea
- ◯ thyme
- ◯ tobacco

PUNGENT
- ◯ burnt match
- ◯ gasoline
- ◯ skunk
- ◯ wet wool
- ◯ whiskey

OTHER

STYLE
Choose One

- ◯ Neat
- ◯ With Water
- ◯ Cocktail

COLOR
Circle One

TASTING WHEEL
Rate your tasting experience, 1 (lowest) to 5 (highest)

Legs, Body, Balance, Sweet, Citrusy, Spicy, Earthy, Nutty, Woody, Smoky, Floral, Herbal, Pungency, Bite, Finish, Linger

TASTING NOTES

Describe the First Sip

....

....

....

Describe the Third Sip

....

....

....

Describe the Body and Finish

....

....

....

What Is Most Striking About This Tequila?

....

....

....

Additional Notes

....

....

....

....

GUIDED TASTING

Write It Out

QUALITY RATING

☆ ☆ ☆ ☆ ☆

COST RATING

OVERALL RATING

RATE IT

Fill It In

TEQUILA
The Details

Brand Name .... Distiller ....

Age .... ABV/Proof .... Date

Distiller's Location .... Price per Glass/Bottle .... Tasting Location

NOSE
Choose All That Apply

SWEET
- ○ brown sugar
- ○ butterscotch
- ○ caramel/toffee
- ○ chocolate
- ○ gingerbread
- ○ honey
- ○ maple syrup
- ○ molasses

FRUITY
- ○ apple

- ○ berry
- ○ cherry
- ○ coconut
- ○ dark fruit
- ○ grapefruit
- ○ lemon
- ○ lime
- ○ peach
- ○ pineapple

WOODY & NUTTY
- ○ almond

- ○ char
- ○ coffee
- ○ oak
- ○ roasted nuts
- ○ smoke

VEGETAL & SPICY
- ○ anise
- ○ asparagus
- ○ black pepper
- ○ cinnamon
- ○ clove

- ○ dill
- ○ gardenia
- ○ geranium
- ○ grass
- ○ jasmine
- ○ lavender
- ○ menthol
- ○ nutmeg
- ○ pepper
- ○ rose
- ○ rosemary

- ○ tea
- ○ thyme
- ○ tobacco

PUNGENT
- ○ burnt match
- ○ gasoline
- ○ skunk
- ○ wet wool
- ○ whiskey

OTHER
....

STYLE
Choose One

- ○ Neat
- ○ With Water
- ○ Cocktail

COLOR
Circle One

TASTING WHEEL
Rate your tasting experience, 1 (lowest) to 5 (highest)

TASTING NOTES

Describe the First Sip

....

....

....

Describe the Third Sip

....

....

....

Describe the Body and Finish

....

....

....

What Is Most Striking About This Tequila?

....

....

....

Additional Notes

....

....

....

....

GUIDED TASTING
Write It Out

QUALITY RATING

☆ ☆ ☆ ☆ ☆

COST RATING

OVERALL RATING

RATE IT
Fill It In

TEQUILA
The Details

Brand Name

Distiller

Age

ABV/Proof

Date

Distiller's Location

Price per Glass/Bottle

Tasting Location

NOSE
Choose All That Apply

SWEET
- ○ brown sugar
- ○ butterscotch
- ○ caramel/toffee
- ○ chocolate
- ○ gingerbread
- ○ honey
- ○ maple syrup
- ○ molasses

FRUITY
- ○ apple

- ○ berry
- ○ cherry
- ○ coconut
- ○ dark fruit
- ○ grapefruit
- ○ lemon
- ○ lime
- ○ peach
- ○ pineapple

WOODY & NUTTY
- ○ almond

- ○ char
- ○ coffee
- ○ oak
- ○ roasted nuts
- ○ smoke

VEGETAL & SPICY
- ○ anise
- ○ asparagus
- ○ black pepper
- ○ cinnamon
- ○ clove

- ○ dill
- ○ gardenia
- ○ geranium
- ○ grass
- ○ jasmine
- ○ lavender
- ○ menthol
- ○ nutmeg
- ○ pepper
- ○ rose
- ○ rosemary

- ○ tea
- ○ thyme
- ○ tobacco

PUNGENT
- ○ burnt match
- ○ gasoline
- ○ skunk
- ○ wet wool
- ○ whiskey

OTHER

STYLE
Choose One

- ○ Neat
- ○ With Water
- ○ Cocktail

COLOR
Circle One

TASTING WHEEL

Rate your tasting experience, 1 (lowest) to 5 (highest)

Legs, Body, Balance, Sweet, Citrusy, Spicy, Earthy, Nutty, Woody, Smoky, Floral, Herbal, Pungency, Bite, Finish, Linger

TASTING NOTES

Describe the First Sip

....

....

....

Describe the Third Sip

....

....

....

Describe the Body and Finish

....

....

....

What Is Most Striking About This Tequila?

....

....

....

Additional Notes

....

....

....

....

QUALITY RATING

☆ ☆ ☆ ☆ ☆

COST RATING

OVERALL RATING

ENJOYING TEQUILA

TEQUILA
The Details

Brand Name   Distiller

Age   ABV/Proof   Date

Distiller's Location   Price per Glass/Bottle   Tasting Location

NOSE
Choose All That Apply

SWEET
- ◯ brown sugar
- ◯ butterscotch
- ◯ caramel/toffee
- ◯ chocolate
- ◯ gingerbread
- ◯ honey
- ◯ maple syrup
- ◯ molasses

FRUITY
- ◯ apple

- ◯ berry
- ◯ cherry
- ◯ coconut
- ◯ dark fruit
- ◯ grapefruit
- ◯ lemon
- ◯ lime
- ◯ peach
- ◯ pineapple

WOODY & NUTTY
- ◯ almond

- ◯ char
- ◯ coffee
- ◯ oak
- ◯ roasted nuts
- ◯ smoke

VEGETAL & SPICY
- ◯ anise
- ◯ asparagus
- ◯ black pepper
- ◯ cinnamon
- ◯ clove

- ◯ dill
- ◯ gardenia
- ◯ geranium
- ◯ grass
- ◯ jasmine
- ◯ lavender
- ◯ menthol
- ◯ nutmeg
- ◯ pepper
- ◯ rose
- ◯ rosemary

- ◯ tea
- ◯ thyme
- ◯ tobacco

PUNGENT
- ◯ burnt match
- ◯ gasoline
- ◯ skunk
- ◯ wet wool
- ◯ whiskey

OTHER
....

STYLE
Choose One

- ◯ Neat
- ◯ With Water
- ◯ Cocktail

COLOR
Circle One

TASTING WHEEL

Rate your tasting experience, 1 (lowest) to 5 (highest)

TASTING NOTES

Describe the First Sip

....

....

....

Describe the Third Sip

....

....

....

Describe the Body and Finish

....

....

....

What Is Most Striking About This Tequila?

....

....

....

Additional Notes

....

....

....

....

GUIDED TASTING

Write It Out

QUALITY RATING

☆ ☆ ☆ ☆ ☆

COST RATING

OVERALL RATING

RATE IT

Fill It In

TEQUILA
The Details

Brand Name

Distiller

Age

ABV/Proof

Date

Distiller's Location

Price per Glass/Bottle

Tasting Location

NOSE
Choose All That Apply

SWEET
- ○ brown sugar
- ○ butterscotch
- ○ caramel/toffee
- ○ chocolate
- ○ gingerbread
- ○ honey
- ○ maple syrup
- ○ molasses

FRUITY
- ○ apple

- ○ berry
- ○ cherry
- ○ coconut
- ○ dark fruit
- ○ grapefruit
- ○ lemon
- ○ lime
- ○ peach
- ○ pineapple

WOODY & NUTTY
- ○ almond

- ○ char
- ○ coffee
- ○ oak
- ○ roasted nuts
- ○ smoke

VEGETAL & SPICY
- ○ anise
- ○ asparagus
- ○ black pepper
- ○ cinnamon
- ○ clove

- ○ dill
- ○ gardenia
- ○ geranium
- ○ grass
- ○ jasmine
- ○ lavender
- ○ menthol
- ○ nutmeg
- ○ pepper
- ○ rose
- ○ rosemary

- ○ tea
- ○ thyme
- ○ tobacco

PUNGENT
- ○ burnt match
- ○ gasoline
- ○ skunk
- ○ wet wool
- ○ whiskey

OTHER

STYLE
Choose One

- ○ Neat
- ○ With Water
- ○ Cocktail

COLOR
Circle One

TASTING WHEEL

Rate your tasting experience, 1 (lowest) to 5 (highest)

TASTING NOTES

Describe the First Sip

....

....

....

Describe the Third Sip

....

....

....

Describe the Body and Finish

....

....

....

What Is Most Striking About This Tequila?

....

....

....

Additional Notes

....

....

....

....

QUALITY RATING	COST RATING	OVERALL RATING
☆ ☆ ☆ ☆ ☆	⑤ ⑤ ⑤ ⑤ ⑤	

TEQUILA
The Details

Brand Name   **Distiller**

Age   **ABV/Proof**   **Date**

Distiller's Location   **Price per Glass/Bottle**   **Tasting Location**

NOSE
Choose All That Apply

SWEET
- brown sugar
- butterscotch
- caramel/toffee
- chocolate
- gingerbread
- honey
- maple syrup
- molasses

FRUITY
- apple

- berry
- cherry
- coconut
- dark fruit
- grapefruit
- lemon
- lime
- peach
- pineapple

WOODY & NUTTY
- almond

- char
- coffee
- oak
- roasted nuts
- smoke

VEGETAL & SPICY
- anise
- asparagus
- black pepper
- cinnamon
- clove

- dill
- gardenia
- geranium
- grass
- jasmine
- lavender
- menthol
- nutmeg
- pepper
- rose
- rosemary

- tea
- thyme
- tobacco

PUNGENT
- burnt match
- gasoline
- skunk
- wet wool
- whiskey

OTHER

STYLE
Choose One

- Neat
- With Water
- Cocktail

COLOR
Circle One

TASTING WHEEL

Rate your tasting experience, 1 (lowest) to 5 (highest)

Legs, Body, Balance, Sweet, Citrusy, Spicy, Earthy, Nutty, Woody, Smoky, Floral, Herbal, Pungency, Bite, Finish, Linger

TASTING NOTES

Describe the First Sip

....
....
....

Describe the Third Sip

....
....
....

Describe the Body and Finish

....
....
....

What Is Most Striking About This Tequila?

....
....
....

Additional Notes

....
....
....
....

GUIDED TASTING

Write It Out

QUALITY RATING

☆ ☆ ☆ ☆ ☆

COST RATING

OVERALL RATING

RATE IT

Fill It In

TEQUILA
The Details

Brand Name

Distiller

Age

ABV/Proof

Date

Distiller's Location

Price per Glass/Bottle

Tasting Location

NOSE
Choose All That Apply

SWEET
- ⚪ brown sugar
- ⚪ butterscotch
- ⚪ caramel/toffee
- ⚪ chocolate
- ⚪ gingerbread
- ⚪ honey
- ⚪ maple syrup
- ⚪ molasses

FRUITY
- ⚪ apple

- ⚪ berry
- ⚪ cherry
- ⚪ coconut
- ⚪ dark fruit
- ⚪ grapefruit
- ⚪ lemon
- ⚪ lime
- ⚪ peach
- ⚪ pineapple

WOODY & NUTTY
- ⚪ almond

- ⚪ char
- ⚪ coffee
- ⚪ oak
- ⚪ roasted nuts
- ⚪ smoke

VEGETAL & SPICY
- ⚪ anise
- ⚪ asparagus
- ⚪ black pepper
- ⚪ cinnamon
- ⚪ clove

- ⚪ dill
- ⚪ gardenia
- ⚪ geranium
- ⚪ grass
- ⚪ jasmine
- ⚪ lavender
- ⚪ menthol
- ⚪ nutmeg
- ⚪ pepper
- ⚪ rose
- ⚪ rosemary

- ⚪ tea
- ⚪ thyme
- ⚪ tobacco

PUNGENT
- ⚪ burnt match
- ⚪ gasoline
- ⚪ skunk
- ⚪ wet wool
- ⚪ whiskey

OTHER

STYLE
Choose One

- ⚪ Neat
- ⚪ With Water
- ⚪ Cocktail

COLOR
Circle One

TASTING WHEEL

Rate your tasting experience, 1 (lowest) to 5 (highest)

Legs, Body, Balance, Sweet, Citrusy, Spicy, Earthy, Nutty, Woody, Smoky, Floral, Herbal, Pungency, Bite, Finish, Linger

TASTING NOTES

Describe the First Sip

....

....

....

Describe the Third Sip

....

....

....

Describe the Body and Finish

....

....

....

What Is Most Striking About This Tequila?

....

....

....

Additional Notes

....

....

....

....

GUIDED TASTING

Write It Out

QUALITY RATING	COST RATING	OVERALL RATING	

RATE IT

Fill It In

TEQUILA
The Details

Brand Name .... Distiller ....

Age .... ABV/Proof .... Date ....

Distiller's Location .... Price per Glass/Bottle .... Tasting Location

NOSE
Choose All That Apply

SWEET
- ○ brown sugar
- ○ butterscotch
- ○ caramel/toffee
- ○ chocolate
- ○ gingerbread
- ○ honey
- ○ maple syrup
- ○ molasses

FRUITY
- ○ apple

- ○ berry
- ○ cherry
- ○ coconut
- ○ dark fruit
- ○ grapefruit
- ○ lemon
- ○ lime
- ○ peach
- ○ pineapple

WOODY & NUTTY
- ○ almond

- ○ char
- ○ coffee
- ○ oak
- ○ roasted nuts
- ○ smoke

VEGETAL & SPICY
- ○ anise
- ○ asparagus
- ○ black pepper
- ○ cinnamon
- ○ clove

- ○ dill
- ○ gardenia
- ○ geranium
- ○ grass
- ○ jasmine
- ○ lavender
- ○ menthol
- ○ nutmeg
- ○ pepper
- ○ rose
- ○ rosemary

- ○ tea
- ○ thyme
- ○ tobacco

PUNGENT
- ○ burnt match
- ○ gasoline
- ○ skunk
- ○ wet wool
- ○ whiskey

OTHER
....

STYLE
Choose One

- ○ Neat
- ○ With Water
- ○ Cocktail

COLOR
Circle One

TASTING WHEEL

Rate your tasting experience, 1 (lowest) to 5 (highest)

TASTING NOTES

Describe the First Sip

....
....
....

Describe the Third Sip

....
....
....

Describe the Body and Finish

....
....
....

What Is Most Striking About This Tequila?

....
....
....

Additional Notes

....
....
....
....

GUIDED TASTING

Write It Out

QUALITY RATING

☆☆☆☆☆

COST RATING

OVERALL RATING

🍾🍾🍾🍾🍾

RATE IT

Fill It In

TEQUILA
The Details

Brand Name   Distiller

Age   ABV/Proof   Date

Distiller's Location   Price per Glass/Bottle   Tasting Location

NOSE
Choose All That Apply

SWEET
- O brown sugar
- O butterscotch
- O caramel/toffee
- O chocolate
- O gingerbread
- O honey
- O maple syrup
- O molasses

FRUITY
- O apple

- O berry
- O cherry
- O coconut
- O dark fruit
- O grapefruit
- O lemon
- O lime
- O peach
- O pineapple

WOODY & NUTTY
- O almond

- O char
- O coffee
- O oak
- O roasted nuts
- O smoke

VEGETAL & SPICY
- O anise
- O asparagus
- O black pepper
- O cinnamon
- O clove

- O dill
- O gardenia
- O geranium
- O grass
- O jasmine
- O lavender
- O menthol
- O nutmeg
- O pepper
- O rose
- O rosemary

- O tea
- O thyme
- O tobacco

PUNGENT
- O burnt match
- O gasoline
- O skunk
- O wet wool
- O whiskey

OTHER

STYLE
Choose One

- O Neat
- O With Water
- O Cocktail

COLOR
Circle One

TASTING WHEEL

Rate your tasting experience, 1 (lowest) to 5 (highest)

Legs, Body, Balance, Sweet, Citrusy, Spicy, Earthy, Nutty, Woody, Smoky, Floral, Herbal, Pungency, Bite, Finish, Linger

TASTING NOTES

Describe the First Sip

....

....

....

Describe the Third Sip

....

....

....

Describe the Body and Finish

....

....

....

What Is Most Striking About This Tequila?

....

....

....

Additional Notes

....

....

....

....

GUIDED TASTING

Write It Out

QUALITY RATING

COST RATING

OVERALL RATING

RATE IT

Fill It In

TEQUILA
The Details

Brand Name

Distiller

Age

ABV/Proof

Date

Distiller's Location

Price per Glass/Bottle

Tasting Location

NOSE
Choose All That Apply

SWEET
- ◯ brown sugar
- ◯ butterscotch
- ◯ caramel/toffee
- ◯ chocolate
- ◯ gingerbread
- ◯ honey
- ◯ maple syrup
- ◯ molasses

FRUITY
- ◯ apple

- ◯ berry
- ◯ cherry
- ◯ coconut
- ◯ dark fruit
- ◯ grapefruit
- ◯ lemon
- ◯ lime
- ◯ peach
- ◯ pineapple

WOODY & NUTTY
- ◯ almond

- ◯ char
- ◯ coffee
- ◯ oak
- ◯ roasted nuts
- ◯ smoke

VEGETAL & SPICY
- ◯ anise
- ◯ asparagus
- ◯ black pepper
- ◯ cinnamon
- ◯ clove

- ◯ dill
- ◯ gardenia
- ◯ geranium
- ◯ grass
- ◯ jasmine
- ◯ lavender
- ◯ menthol
- ◯ nutmeg
- ◯ pepper
- ◯ rose
- ◯ rosemary

- ◯ tea
- ◯ thyme
- ◯ tobacco

PUNGENT
- ◯ burnt match
- ◯ gasoline
- ◯ skunk
- ◯ wet wool
- ◯ whiskey

OTHER
....

STYLE
Choose One

- ◯ Neat
- ◯ With Water
- ◯ Cocktail

COLOR
Circle One

TASTING WHEEL

Rate your tasting experience, 1 (lowest) to 5 (highest)

Legs, Body, Balance, Sweet, Citrusy, Spicy, Earthy, Nutty, Woody, Smoky, Floral, Herbal, Pungency, Bite, Finish, Linger

TASTING NOTES

Describe the First Sip

....

....

....

Describe the Third Sip

....

....

....

Describe the Body and Finish

....

....

....

What Is Most Striking About This Tequila?

....

....

....

Additional Notes

....

....

....

....

GUIDED TASTING

Write It Out

QUALITY RATING

 ☆ ☆ ☆ ☆ ☆

COST RATING

 ⑤ ⑤ ⑤ ⑤ ⑤

OVERALL RATING

RATE IT

Fill It In

TEQUILA
The Details

Brand Name   **Distiller**

Age   **ABV/Proof**   **Date**

Distiller's Location   **Price per Glass/Bottle**   **Tasting Location**

NOSE
Choose All That Apply

SWEET
- ○ brown sugar
- ○ butterscotch
- ○ caramel/toffee
- ○ chocolate
- ○ gingerbread
- ○ honey
- ○ maple syrup
- ○ molasses

FRUITY
- ○ apple

- ○ berry
- ○ cherry
- ○ coconut
- ○ dark fruit
- ○ grapefruit
- ○ lemon
- ○ lime
- ○ peach
- ○ pineapple

WOODY & NUTTY
- ○ almond

- ○ char
- ○ coffee
- ○ oak
- ○ roasted nuts
- ○ smoke

VEGETAL & SPICY
- ○ anise
- ○ asparagus
- ○ black pepper
- ○ cinnamon
- ○ clove

- ○ dill
- ○ gardenia
- ○ geranium
- ○ grass
- ○ jasmine
- ○ lavender
- ○ menthol
- ○ nutmeg
- ○ pepper
- ○ rose
- ○ rosemary

- ○ tea
- ○ thyme
- ○ tobacco

PUNGENT
- ○ burnt match
- ○ gasoline
- ○ skunk
- ○ wet wool
- ○ whiskey

OTHER

STYLE
Choose One

- ○ Neat
- ○ With Water
- ○ Cocktail

COLOR
Circle One

TASTING WHEEL

Rate your tasting experience, 1 (lowest) to 5 (highest)

Legs · Linger · Body · Finish · Balance · Bite · Sweet · Pungency · Citrusy · Herbal · Spicy · Floral · Earthy · Smoky · Woody · Nutty

TASTING NOTES

Describe the First Sip

....

....

....

Describe the Third Sip

....

....

....

Describe the Body and Finish

....

....

....

What Is Most Striking About This Tequila?

....

....

....

Additional Notes

....

....

....

....

QUALITY RATING	COST RATING	OVERALL RATING
☆☆☆☆☆		

TEQUILA
The Details

Brand Name

Distiller

Age

ABV/Proof

Date

Distiller's Location

Price per Glass/Bottle

Tasting Location

NOSE
Choose All That Apply

SWEET
- ○ brown sugar
- ○ butterscotch
- ○ caramel/toffee
- ○ chocolate
- ○ gingerbread
- ○ honey
- ○ maple syrup
- ○ molasses

FRUITY
- ○ apple

- ○ berry
- ○ cherry
- ○ coconut
- ○ dark fruit
- ○ grapefruit
- ○ lemon
- ○ lime
- ○ peach
- ○ pineapple

WOODY & NUTTY
- ○ almond

- ○ char
- ○ coffee
- ○ oak
- ○ roasted nuts
- ○ smoke

VEGETAL & SPICY
- ○ anise
- ○ asparagus
- ○ black pepper
- ○ cinnamon
- ○ clove

- ○ dill
- ○ gardenia
- ○ geranium
- ○ grass
- ○ jasmine
- ○ lavender
- ○ menthol
- ○ nutmeg
- ○ pepper
- ○ rose
- ○ rosemary

- ○ tea
- ○ thyme
- ○ tobacco

PUNGENT
- ○ burnt match
- ○ gasoline
- ○ skunk
- ○ wet wool
- ○ whiskey

OTHER

STYLE
Choose One

- ○ Neat
- ○ With Water
- ○ Cocktail

COLOR
Circle One

TASTING WHEEL

Rate your tasting experience, 1 (lowest) to 5 (highest)

TASTING NOTES

Describe the First Sip

....

....

....

Describe the Third Sip

....

....

....

Describe the Body and Finish

....

....

....

What Is Most Striking About This Tequila?

....

....

....

Additional Notes

....

....

....

....

GUIDED TASTING

Write It Out

QUALITY RATING	COST RATING	OVERALL RATING
☆☆☆☆☆		

RATE IT

Fill It In

ENJOYING TEQUILA

Brand Name   **Distiller**

Age   **ABV/Proof**   **Date**

Distiller's Location   **Price per Glass/Bottle**   **Tasting Location**

NOSE
Choose All That Apply

SWEET
- ○ brown sugar
- ○ butterscotch
- ○ caramel/toffee
- ○ chocolate
- ○ gingerbread
- ○ honey
- ○ maple syrup
- ○ molasses

FRUITY
- ○ apple
- ○ berry
- ○ cherry
- ○ coconut
- ○ dark fruit
- ○ grapefruit
- ○ lemon
- ○ lime
- ○ peach
- ○ pineapple

WOODY & NUTTY
- ○ almond
- ○ char
- ○ coffee
- ○ oak
- ○ roasted nuts
- ○ smoke

VEGETAL & SPICY
- ○ anise
- ○ asparagus
- ○ black pepper
- ○ cinnamon
- ○ clove
- ○ dill
- ○ gardenia
- ○ geranium
- ○ grass
- ○ jasmine
- ○ lavender
- ○ menthol
- ○ nutmeg
- ○ pepper
- ○ rose
- ○ rosemary
- ○ tea
- ○ thyme
- ○ tobacco

PUNGENT
- ○ burnt match
- ○ gasoline
- ○ skunk
- ○ wet wool
- ○ whiskey

OTHER

STYLE
Choose One

- ○ Neat
- ○ With Water
- ○ Cocktail

TASTING WHEEL

Rate your tasting experience, 1 (lowest) to 5 (highest)

Legs · Linger · Body · Finish · Balance · Bite · Sweet · Pungency · Citrusy · Herbal · Spicy · Floral · Earthy · Smoky · Woody · Nutty

COLOR
Circle One

TASTING NOTES

Describe the First Sip

....

....

....

Describe the Third Sip

....

....

....

Describe the Body and Finish

....

....

....

What Is Most Striking About This Tequila?

....

....

....

Additional Notes

....

....

....

....

....

GUIDED TASTING
Write It Out

QUALITY RATING	COST RATING	OVERALL RATING

RATE IT
Fill It In

ENJOYING TEQUILA

TEQUILA
The Details

Brand Name .... Distiller ....

Age .... ABV/Proof .... Date ....

Distiller's Location .... Price per Glass/Bottle .... Tasting Location ....

NOSE
Choose All That Apply

SWEET
- ○ brown sugar
- ○ butterscotch
- ○ caramel/toffee
- ○ chocolate
- ○ gingerbread
- ○ honey
- ○ maple syrup
- ○ molasses

FRUITY
- ○ apple

- ○ berry
- ○ cherry
- ○ coconut
- ○ dark fruit
- ○ grapefruit
- ○ lemon
- ○ lime
- ○ peach
- ○ pineapple

WOODY & NUTTY
- ○ almond

- ○ char
- ○ coffee
- ○ oak
- ○ roasted nuts
- ○ smoke

VEGETAL & SPICY
- ○ anise
- ○ asparagus
- ○ black pepper
- ○ cinnamon
- ○ clove

- ○ dill
- ○ gardenia
- ○ geranium
- ○ grass
- ○ jasmine
- ○ lavender
- ○ menthol
- ○ nutmeg
- ○ pepper
- ○ rose
- ○ rosemary

- ○ tea
- ○ thyme
- ○ tobacco

PUNGENT
- ○ burnt match
- ○ gasoline
- ○ skunk
- ○ wet wool
- ○ whiskey

OTHER
....

STYLE
Choose One

- ○ Neat
- ○ With Water
- ○ Cocktail

COLOR
Circle One

TASTING WHEEL

Rate your tasting experience, 1 (lowest) to 5 (highest)

TASTING NOTES

GUIDED TASTING

Describe the First Sip

....

....

....

Describe the Third Sip

....

....

....

Describe the Body and Finish

....

....

....

What Is Most Striking About This Tequila?

....

....

....

Additional Notes

....

....

....

....

GUIDED TASTING

Write It Out

QUALITY RATING

☆ ☆ ☆ ☆ ☆

COST RATING

OVERALL RATING

RATE IT

Fill It In

ENJOYING TEQUILA

TEQUILA
The Details

Brand Name .... Distiller ....

Age .... ABV/Proof .... Date ....

Distiller's Location .... Price per Glass/Bottle .... Tasting Location ....

NOSE
Choose All That Apply

SWEET
- ◯ brown sugar
- ◯ butterscotch
- ◯ caramel/toffee
- ◯ chocolate
- ◯ gingerbread
- ◯ honey
- ◯ maple syrup
- ◯ molasses

FRUITY
- ◯ apple

- ◯ berry
- ◯ cherry
- ◯ coconut
- ◯ dark fruit
- ◯ grapefruit
- ◯ lemon
- ◯ lime
- ◯ peach
- ◯ pineapple

WOODY & NUTTY
- ◯ almond

- ◯ char
- ◯ coffee
- ◯ oak
- ◯ roasted nuts
- ◯ smoke

VEGETAL & SPICY
- ◯ anise
- ◯ asparagus
- ◯ black pepper
- ◯ cinnamon
- ◯ clove

- ◯ dill
- ◯ gardenia
- ◯ geranium
- ◯ grass
- ◯ jasmine
- ◯ lavender
- ◯ menthol
- ◯ nutmeg
- ◯ pepper
- ◯ rose
- ◯ rosemary

- ◯ tea
- ◯ thyme
- ◯ tobacco

PUNGENT
- ◯ burnt match
- ◯ gasoline
- ◯ skunk
- ◯ wet wool
- ◯ whiskey

OTHER
....

STYLE
Choose One

- ◯ Neat
- ◯ With Water
- ◯ Cocktail

COLOR
Circle One

TASTING WHEEL

Rate your tasting experience, 1 (lowest) to 5 (highest)

Legs · Body · Balance · Sweet · Citrusy · Spicy · Earthy · Nutty · Woody · Smoky · Floral · Herbal · Pungency · Bite · Finish · Linger

TASTING NOTES

Describe the First Sip

....
....
....

Describe the Third Sip

....
....
....

Describe the Body and Finish

....
....
....

What Is Most Striking About This Tequila?

....
....
....

Additional Notes

....
....
....
....

GUIDED TASTING

Write It Out

QUALITY RATING **COST RATING** **OVERALL RATING**

RATE IT

Fill It In

ENJOYING TEQUILA

TEQUILA
The Details

Brand Name .... **Distiller**

Age .... **ABV/Proof** .... **Date**

Distiller's Location .... **Price per Glass/Bottle** .... **Tasting Location**

NOSE
Choose All That Apply

SWEET
- ○ brown sugar
- ○ butterscotch
- ○ caramel/toffee
- ○ chocolate
- ○ gingerbread
- ○ honey
- ○ maple syrup
- ○ molasses

FRUITY
- ○ apple
- ○ berry
- ○ cherry
- ○ coconut
- ○ dark fruit
- ○ grapefruit
- ○ lemon
- ○ lime
- ○ peach
- ○ pineapple

WOODY & NUTTY
- ○ almond
- ○ char
- ○ coffee
- ○ oak
- ○ roasted nuts
- ○ smoke

VEGETAL & SPICY
- ○ anise
- ○ asparagus
- ○ black pepper
- ○ cinnamon
- ○ clove
- ○ dill
- ○ gardenia
- ○ geranium
- ○ grass
- ○ jasmine
- ○ lavender
- ○ menthol
- ○ nutmeg
- ○ pepper
- ○ rose
- ○ rosemary
- ○ tea
- ○ thyme
- ○ tobacco

PUNGENT
- ○ burnt match
- ○ gasoline
- ○ skunk
- ○ wet wool
- ○ whiskey

OTHER
....

STYLE
Choose One
- ○ Neat
- ○ With Water
- ○ Cocktail

COLOR
Circle One

TASTING WHEEL
Rate your tasting experience, 1 (lowest) to 5 (highest)

TASTING NOTES

Describe the First Sip

....

....

....

Describe the Third Sip

....

....

....

Describe the Body and Finish

....

....

....

What Is Most Striking About This Tequila?

....

....

....

Additional Notes

....

....

....

....

GUIDED TASTING

Write It Out

QUALITY RATING

☆ ☆ ☆ ☆ ☆

COST RATING

OVERALL RATING

RATE IT

Fill It In

ENJOYING TEQUILA

TEQUILA
The Details

Brand Name

Distiller

Age

ABV/Proof

Date

Distiller's Location

Price per Glass/Bottle

Tasting Location

NOSE
Choose All That Apply

SWEET
- ○ brown sugar
- ○ butterscotch
- ○ caramel/toffee
- ○ chocolate
- ○ gingerbread
- ○ honey
- ○ maple syrup
- ○ molasses

FRUITY
- ○ apple

- ○ berry
- ○ cherry
- ○ coconut
- ○ dark fruit
- ○ grapefruit
- ○ lemon
- ○ lime
- ○ peach
- ○ pineapple

WOODY & NUTTY
- ○ almond

- ○ char
- ○ coffee
- ○ oak
- ○ roasted nuts
- ○ smoke

VEGETAL & SPICY
- ○ anise
- ○ asparagus
- ○ black pepper
- ○ cinnamon
- ○ clove

- ○ dill
- ○ gardenia
- ○ geranium
- ○ grass
- ○ jasmine
- ○ lavender
- ○ menthol
- ○ nutmeg
- ○ pepper
- ○ rose
- ○ rosemary

- ○ tea
- ○ thyme
- ○ tobacco

PUNGENT
- ○ burnt match
- ○ gasoline
- ○ skunk
- ○ wet wool
- ○ whiskey

OTHER

STYLE
Choose One

- ○ Neat
- ○ With Water
- ○ Cocktail

COLOR
Circle One

TASTING WHEEL

Rate your tasting experience, 1 (lowest) to 5 (highest)

TASTING NOTES

Describe the First Sip

....

....

....

Describe the Third Sip

....

....

....

Describe the Body and Finish

....

....

....

What Is Most Striking About This Tequila?

....

....

....

Additional Notes

....

....

....

....

QUALITY RATING	COST RATING	OVERALL RATING

RATE IT

Fill It In

INDEX

IMAGE CREDITS